February 19, 1978

$12.95

african cichlids
of lakes malawi
and tanganyika

Labeotropheus trewavasae. Photo courtesy Wardley Products Co.

by dr. herbert r. axelrod
and warren e. burgess

SIXTH EDITION,
REVISED AND ENLARGED

Cover: *Melanochromis* sp. (top) and *Trematocranus jacobfreibergi* (below).

Photos in this book, unless otherwise credited, are by Dr. Herbert R. Axelrod.

First Edition
©1973 by T.F.H. Publications, Inc. Ltd.
Second Edition, Revised and Enlarged
©1974 by T.F.H. Publications, Inc. Ltd.
Third Edition, Revised and Enlarged
©1975 by T.F.H. Publications, Inc. Ltd.
Fourth Edition, Revised and Enlarged
©1976 by T.F.H. Publications, Inc. Ltd.
Fifth Edition, Revised and Enlarged
©1976 by T.F.H. Publications, Inc. Ltd.
Sixth Edition, Revised and Enlarged
©1977 by T.F.H. Publications, Inc. Ltd.

ISBN 0-87666-468-0

Distributed in the U.S.A. by T.F.H. Publications, Inc., 211 West Sylvania Avenue, P.O. Box 27, Neptune City, N.J. 07753; in England by T.F.H. (Gt. Britain) Ltd., 13 Nutley Lane, Reigate, Surrey; in Canada to the book store and library trade by Clarke, Irwin & Company, Clarwin House, 791 St. Clair Avenue West, Toronto 10, Ontario; in Canada to the pet trade by Rolf C. Hagen Ltd., 3225 Sartelon Street, Montreal 382, Quebec; in Southeast Asia by Y.W. Ong, 9 Lorong 36 Geylang, Singapore 14; in Australia and the south Pacific by Pet Imports Pty. Ltd., P.O. Box 149, Brookvale 2100, N.S.W., Australia. Published by T.F.H. Publications, Inc. Ltd., The British Crown Colony of Hong Kong.

Printed in the U.S.A.

TABLE OF CONTENTS

Back Row: Warren E. Burgess, Dr. Herbert R. Axelrod, Glen Axelrod. *Front Row:* Henny and Peter Davies. Photo by Evelyn Axelrod.

DEDICATION

This book is dedicated to Peter and Henny Davies of Cape McClear, Lake Malawi for all the beautiful fishes they found and made available for aquarists.

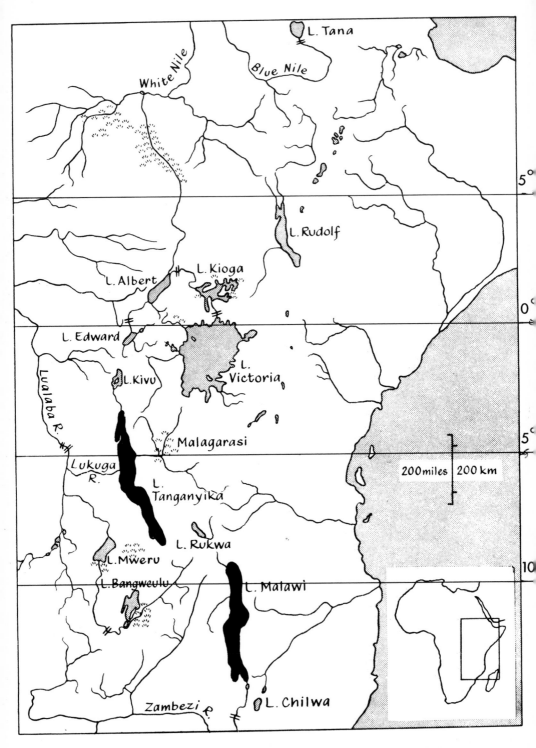

The great lakes of East Africa, with the major associated river systems, and barriers—waterfalls and rapids—which have been and are important in the isolation of various basins.

Introduction

It was not more than 100 years ago that the first Europeans discovered the great lakes of Africa, but since that time there have been numerous expeditions and quantities of scientific studies dealing with Lakes Victoria, Nyasa (Malawi) and Tanganyika. Foremost of the scientists writing about these lakes are Dr. Ethelwynn Trewavas of the British Museum and her associate Dr. P. H. Greenwood, Dr. Geoffrey Fryer, and Dr. Max Poll.

The fishes of Lakes Malawi and Tanganyika are of special interest to aquarists because there are hundreds of interesting cichlids which are found only in these lakes; many of these cichlids are richly colored and have interesting feeding and breeding habits.

Both of these lakes are being exploited for their aquarium fishes by active, dependable collectors who have long experience in fish collecting and who practice sound principles of conservation. Specifically, Pierre Brichard, working out of Bujumbura, Burundi, sends out about 100 boxes (about 5000 fishes) per week of mostly Tanganyikan cichlids; in Malawi Peter Davies, along with his wife Henny, ships about the same quantity of mainly Malawian cichlids. It is to these two gentlemen that the aquarium world owes a great deal of thanks, for without their perseverance and dedication, few fishes, if any, would ever grace our tanks.

The sketch and caption were taken from Fryer and Iles' *"The Cichlid Fishes of the Great Lakes of Africa."*

7

Aerial view of Lake Malawi about 10 miles from Monkey Bay
at a height of 800 feet.

Lake Malawi has islands which remind the author of oceanic coral islands, and peninsulas such as this one, which provide habitats for the many cichlids found there.

1

The Lakes

Lakes Tanganyika and Malawi are large lakes, being the seventh and ninth largest lakes in the world. Tanganyika has an area of 34,000 square kilometres (13,124 square miles), while Malawi has an area of about 30,000 square kilometers (11,430 square miles). Lake Malawi reaches a depth of about 750 metres, almost half a mile, while Lake Tanganyika is almost 1500 meters deep, or almost a mile. The acidity, or rather alkalinity, of the lakes' waters varies. Lake Malawi's pH value fluctuates between 7.7 and 8.6, while Tanganyika is much more alkaline, with its pH varying between 8.6 and 9.2. This is important information for the aquarist, since the fish do not do well in neutral or acid water.

Not all Malawian shores are rocky. Certain areas, shown in the photos above and below, are sandy. Unfortunately the colorful fishes are found among the rocks, where they are much more difficult to capture.

Huge rocks under the water support a ½-inch thick crust of algae which are grazed upon by cichlid fishes. This scene is in 12 feet of water near Cape McClear.

What is so unbelievable is that Lake Malawi has more different species of fishes than any other lake anywhere in the world, while Lake Tanganyika is third in this respect. Lake Victoria, by the way, also one of Africa's great lakes, ranks second.

I do not think of these bodies of water as lakes, because they are so unlike the lakes I know in South America. I prefer to think of these lakes as oceans, because they, like the oceans, contain many islands and almost every island has its own special fauna of cichlid fishes. Surely many of the islands have the same fishes, but more often than not the fishes, although very similar in body form, have different color patterns, and it is quite questionable whether they are truly the same species or whether they are sub-species . . . they might even be distinct species. More scientific work is clearly indicated.

A view of Monkey Bay, Lake Malawi (above), taken from a hill overlooking the bay. Photo by David Eccles. Below is Lake Tanganyika photographed from the Bujumbura, Burundi shore with the Congo (Zaire) Mountains in the background.

Muddy water runs through Tanganyika and Uganda, bringing nutrient salts in the silt to Lake Victoria. Aerial view at 3,000 feet.

Swamplands and marshes also can be found in Lake Malawi. The photo above was taken at 2,000 feet and shows Lake Malawi near Monkey Bay. The lower photo is a closeup of the marshland.

Pierre Brichard searching for Tanganyikan cichlids in about 30 feet of water. Brichard uses an anaesthesia (quinaldine dissolved in acetone) to stun the fish as they hide in the tiny crevices between the rocks.

In 1972 and 1973 I made several expeditions to both lakes, being unable to explore Lake Victoria because of the unfriendly attitude of President Amin of Uganda, who controls Lake Victoria. But I was able to dive in both Lake Malawi and Lake Tanganyika. I can highly recommend diving in those lakes, for their waters are clear and clean and free of the horrible parasite *Schistosoma*, which the Africans call *"Bilharzia,"* an obsolete scientific name. *Schistosoma*, a fluke, is carried by snails.

Diving is relatively safe in these lakes, though the hippos and crocodiles may present a problem at times. I had a close call with a huge electric catfish in Tanganyika, and my diving partner, Thierry Brichard, was almost bitten by a diving cobra which coiled ready to strike . . . underwater!

Lake Malawi, according to Fryer and Iles' magnificent book *The Cichlid Fishes of the Great Lakes of Africa*, contains more than 200 species of cichlids, of which all except 4 are endemic. It has about 42 other species of fishes, of which about 26 are endemic.

18

The tide is seasonal in Lake Malawi, with the lake falling during the dry season and rising during the rainy season. The rings around the rocks give some idea of the tide. Since algae grows only to a fairly low water depth, after which there is not enough light to support plant growth, the low tide season enables algae to grow in areas where it would not normally survive.

During the rainy season water flows out of Lake Tanganyika and Lake Malawi since they are very high in the mountains. Dirty silt-laden water enters the lakes and clean water leaves.

According to Fryer and Iles, Lake Tanganyika has 126 species of cichlids, all endemic, and 67 other fishes of which 47 are endemic. These estimates are conservative as many new species have been discovered since their work was published.

The cichlids of these lakes vary in size from the tiny *Lamprologus kungweensis* of Lake Tanganyika, which measures only $1\frac{1}{2}$ inches in length, to the comparatively enormous *Boulengerochromis microlepis,* which measures about $2\frac{1}{2}$ feet in length. The largest cichlid weighs 800 times more than the smallest!

Since the lakes are fairly deep you would expect cichlids to be found at most depths, but most of the fishes are found in the top 50 feet. The cichlids living at the lower portion of the 50-foot depth range present severe problems in collecting, because fishes found in 50 feet of water or deeper have to be decompressed before they can be safely maintained in aquaria. Cichlids, like most other bony fishes, have a gas-filled swim bladder which must be adjusted slowly to varying depths. Thus a cichlid living at a depth of 50 feet might explode if brought up to the surface

The rock in the foreground is white from bird droppings. This is a typical habitat of mbuna cichlids in Lake Malawi.

Pierre Brichard with his "decompression chamber" for fishes. Brichard found it necessary to decompress all his fishes which were captured at a depth of about 20 feet or more.

too quickly, and in many of our seine hauls we found that in cichlids caught at 50 to 100 feet of depth the swim bladder would be so distended that it pushed the intestines out of the anus. Brichard invented a decompression chamber which was a barrel of about 50-gallon capacity which had a relief valve for the pressure to be slowly adjusted. Cichlids brought up from 25 feet also had swim bladder problems; their buoyancy when brought up swiftly resulted in their struggling belly-up for hours before they could relieve the air pressure in their bladders. One disadvantage of cichlid swim bladders (which are called "physoclistous" swim bladders) is that they have no direct connection to the outside of the fish, and air is secreted and absorbed slowly. Cichlid fishes have been found as deep as 215 meters in Lake Tanganyika.

Can you believe this scene? It is in only 16 feet of water in Lake Tanganyika. The fish in the foreground are *Lamprologus brichardi*; the single fish is *Julidochromis marlieri*.

The four Malawian fishes on this and the facing page were all taken from water over 25 feet deep. They were brought to the surface too quickly and their extended swim bladder is forcing their intestines out of their bodies.

Page 24, top: *Lethrinops gossei* ; page 24, bottom: *Haploch-romis hennydaviesae*; p.25, top: *Haplochromis sphaerodon;* page 25, bottom: *Haplochromis annectens.*

This is a typical habitat of mbuna cichlids in Lake Malawi.

2
Peculiarities of Certain African Cichlids

There is something special about certain cichlids. Many fishes which have physoclistous (sealed) air bladders, develop the "seal" only after they, in their fry stage, have taken a gulp of air to initially fill their bladder with air. Once the bladder is filled, the duct seals itself and the fish no longer requires a visit to the surface. Some cichlids have so progressed that they no longer must take that first gulp of air. This is important because we know that African cichlids always spawn close to the bottom of an aquarium; in the African lakes they are never found spawning near the surface but always on the bottom. They watch and protect their young closely, and if the young had to escape to the surface to catch an air bubble, the parental behavior pattern would be broken. Cichlid fishes exhibit, almost universally, a range of parental care from simple guarding of the eggs and fry to orally incubating the eggs and utilizing their buccal cavity for a safe retreat for their free-swimming offspring.

The spines of fishes have long been utilized by ichthyologists to help identify fishes. Cichlids from all over the world have from 2 to 12 spines in their anal fins, but African cichlids all have 6 anal spines or fewer . . . except for certain cichlids found in Lake Tanganyika. Also, except for one species, the cichlids of Lakes Victoria and Malawi have only 3 anal spines.

Most of the cichlid species of these lakes have interesting teeth which have evolved to become specially suited to certain feeding habits. These feeding habits change as the fishes grow. Certainly adult fishes which prefer other fishes' eyeballs, or which scrape the scales from the tails of even larger species, would hardly be

Compare the shape of the head, mouth and lips of this fish, *Diplotaxodon ecclesi*, with *Lethrinops gossei* on the facing page.

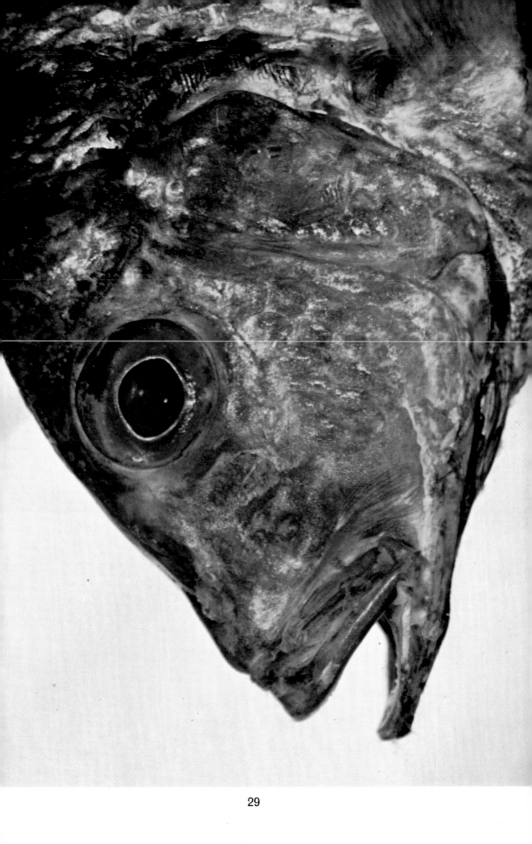

(a) shows a side view of the Malawian eye-eater,

Haplochromis compressiceps; (b) is a closeup of the mouth.
Photos from Fryer and Iles *"The Cichlid Fishes of the Great Lakes of Africa."*

able to have the same diet when they are young and very small. Thus the teeth of a fish are very important only when fishes of the same age and/or size are compared. Many ichthyologists failed to take into account this change in dentition when they described small fishes as being different species.

The mouths of our African cichlids are used for other things besides eating. Like most other teleost fishes, African cichlids "inhale" water through their mouths and squirt it over their 4 pairs of gills in the familiar chewing motion. The gills exchange oxygen for carbon dioxide the same way (more or less) that our own lungs operate. Humans and other mammals do not have to open their mouths to breathe . . . cichlids do. But cichlids also use their mouths, in many cases, for brooding fry and eggs, so this same breathing apparatus enables the developing eggs and fry to be aerated with fresh water automatically as their parent "breathes." Cichlids do, by the way, have nostrils, but these nostrils end in dead-end sacs, and their function is in no way directly connected with breathing.

Like many other fishes, African cichlids show different coloration between adult males and females in many cases. They also have color patterns which manifest themselves during periods of fright or breeding or brooding, and they have nighttime colors and juvenile colors. Probably the juvenile coloration is for camouflage purposes as well as for recognition, because almost certainly the colors of the juveniles are less accentuated than those of a breeding male.

Besides basic overall color, there are certain color patterns in the fins of the fishes. The so called "egg spots" of some of the cichlids has been well publicized by Dr. Wickler, who wrote extensively to show that the egg spots found on the anal fins of the males of mouth brooding species assisted the female of the species to fertilize the eggs in her mouth. Wickler proposed that the female would peck at the egg spots, perhaps thereby stimulating the male to release sperm, thus enabling the female to get a mouthful of sperm with which to fertilize the eggs in her buccal cavity. *I disagree with Wickler.* I propose that the eggs spots are used solely for identification. Cichlids in many cases spawn and court in relatively secret quarters. We know that in the aquarium they prefer dark caves and dig under rocks and logs to spawn as secretly as possible. While diving under huge boulders in Lakes Malawi and Tanganyika, all I could see sometimes were the spots on the anal fins of the males. It was probably too dark for the

In support of his theory on egg spots, Dr. Wickler published the drawing above. The drawing seems to have been made from the photo below by Rudolf Zukal. The scene depicts a female picking up eggs as the male fertilizes them. A close view will indicate the female is not "attacking" the spots at all.

In the darkness under huge boulders in Lake Malawi everything is green and murky. . .except for the glowing identification marks on the anal fins of some mbunas.

The photograph above and those on the facing page show how well the egg spots show up on fishes in the deep and poorly lit areas under the boulders some 20-30 feet deep in Lake Malawi. The author contends these spots are for identification and are not to trick the female into trying to snatch the "eggs" from the male's anal fin.

male to make out prospective mating partners, so they waited for females to come their way. A female probably signals her acceptance by pecking at the male's anal fin spots, thus making it easier for the fish to find each other both initially and during the spawning process. Thus I reject completely the "egg spot" theory of Wickler in favor of my own "color recognition" theory. Fortunately I was able to take some photographs underwater in Lake Malawi to demonstrate my observations.

Cichlids, by the way, can change their colors quickly. I have often caught a brilliantly colored breeding male only to have him fade away after a few moments to a common-looking fish even before I could put him into a photo tank.

Still further proof exists for the rejection of the egg spot theory. There are many color varieties or "morphs" of certain species. Some are striped, some have solid colors, and some are yellow, while their morphs are blue or banded. Those fishes which have

Haplochromis placodon. The female, above, and the male in the lower photograph, show very clearly that this fish has egg spots in every unpaired fin except the anal!! A closeup of the dorsal and caudal fins on the facing page shows typical egg spots which would be unexplainable by the egg spot theory of Dr. Wickler.

Haplochromis sphaerodon is another fish which has egg spots in its dorsal and caudal fins and none in its anal fin. The upper photo is a closeup of the unpaired fins.

Haplochromis taeniolatus, above, has no egg spots at all, while *Hemitilapia oxyrhynchus* has egg spots in the dorsal and caudal but none in the anal fin. All of this evidence has convinced the author that the Wickler egg spot theory must be rejected.

Haplochromis polystigma in breeding dress (above) and in its usual color pattern (below). It is interesting that the egg spots on the anal fin are only visible when the fish is *not* in breeding color.

Haplochromis similis has almost perfect egg spots in its dorsal fin only.

dark morphs always seem to have bright egg spots, while those brighter colored morphs have, at times, no egg spots at all! The brighter fish are never found under rocks but almost always are found alongside or atop rocks . . . the darker fish never spawn in the open.

Further evidence in support of the recognition theory is the behavior manifest when a male sees a ripe female. Almost immediately, the male will spread his fins, fully extending his anal and dorsal fins as well, and begin to "dance" in front of the female, showing as clearly as possible the egg spots and other recognition signs on his fins and body. In many species of African cichlids the unpaired fins (anal, dorsal and caudal) are significantly marked and show more variation between species in many closely related fishes than do meristic (measurable) characteristics.

There are at least four described morphs of *Pseudotropheus zebra.* In the BB morph of Fryer and Iles both sexes have alternating blue and black vertical bars shown in the fish above.

In the B morph the fish are from a sky blue to a mauve in color, sexes being colored alike. This fish, by the way, was photographed in the aquarium in the lobby of the Monkey Bay Hotel of Mr. and Mrs. Otto.

These photos are of one of the original specimens of *Labido-chromis fryeri*. The fish apparently came from Mumbo Island, Lake Malawi and was exhibited in an aquarium in the lobby at the Monkey Bay Hotel.

In the OB morph the fish are orange blotched, a color pattern which is more common for females than for males.

In nature some color patterns seem to overlap and to determine which zebra morph they are is difficult.

Whilst diving in 25 feet of water near Cape McClear, I spotted this *Pseudotropheus* which seems to be a reverse *tropheops* pattern. There were about a dozen fish with this coloration in the area which I visited. Below is a normal *Pseudotropheus tropheops* male.

These two fish are also known as *Pseudotropheus tropheops* sensu Jackson. It is doubtful that they are identical to the fish on the opposite page of the same name even though their meristic characters overlap. When sufficient specimens are available for study it is almost certain these fish will be considered a subspecies or separate species.

These two fish (female holotype above, male paratype below) were discovered in Lake Malawi by Peter and Henny Davies and described as a new species, *Pseudotropheus johanni*, by Eccles. The name was recently changed to *Melanochromis johanni*.

A closeup of the head of the holotype of the recently described *Melanochromis simulans.*

A closeup of the head of the holotype of *Melanochromis johanni.*

The fish above is the recently described *Melanochromis simulans*, so called because of its striking similarity to *Melanochromis auratus* shown below.

I chased this fish into 40 feet of water to take its photograph. It is a morph of *Pseudotropheus tropheops*, but I cannot exactly say which one. Note the poor condition of this fish. Below is a *Labeotropheus trewavasae* which might have had an encounter with a scale eater that chopped off a piece of its caudal fin.

These two fishes are in the "utaka" group taken in fairly deep water by trawl. They belong to the genus *Haplochromis* but I was unable to get a species-positive identification.

3
Rocks and Islands

The aerial views of Lake Malawi show to some degree why it and the other large African lakes remind me of the oceans. The more rocks found in a particular area, the more fishes . . . especially more cichlids, even though not all cichlids by any means are found exclusively around rocks. Many species are found in open water, but in most cases these open water forms cannot be readily caught because of their swim bladder problems when seined from any appreciable depth and because in most cases the deep water forms are not highly colored.

A typical scene in twenty feet of water in Lake Malawi. The number of fishes is staggering . . . but catching them is another story.

The scenes above and below are at 25 feet depth near Cape McClear, Lake Malawi. The rocks are covered with a thin layer of algae which are constantly being grazed upon by various fishes. Note the angle at which the fishes attack the algae and pay attention to the many dark "holes" in which the fishes hide and spawn.

Cyphotilapia frontosa in their typical habitat in Lake Tanganyika.

The cichlids of Lake Malawi found around the rocks have been called *"mbuna"* after the native name used near Nkata Bay. Other areas of Lake Malawi refer to the rock-inhabiting fishes under different names. "Mbuna" is pronounced "mmmmmboona" and not "em-boona" as I have previously written. "Em-boona" is the way a European would pronounce it, being unaccustomed to swallowing the "m" the way Africans do without parting their lips to enunciate the "m."

The basic habitat of the shore fishes of Lakes Malawi and Tanganyika are rocks, grassy or sandy open areas between the rocks and the grass. The accompanying photographs show very well the differences between these habitats, and it is exceedingly rare that mbunas stray from their particular ecological niche. Since the rocky areas, especially the islands, are more or less isolated within the lake, in order for an mbuna to get from one area to another he would have to cross open water. Mbunas refuse to cross open waters.

All of the rocky habitat fishes in both Tanganyika and Malawi insist upon keeping their belly region pointed to the rocks, so

The photographs above and below are taken in 8 feet (lower photo) and 20 feet (upper photo) of water in the sandy, grassy habitats to be found in Lake Malawi. Note the protective coloration of the fishes.

A closer view of the Lake Malawi sandy, grassy habitat which more clearly shows the kinds of fishes found in this habitat. Below is a sandy area in Lake Tanganyika which shows *Cyathopharynx furcifer* circling over their huge nest. The fish in the foreground is *Cyphotilapia frontosa*.

The photographs on these two facing pages should be evaluated for protective coloration. The *Pseudotropheus zebra* BB morph shown in the two top photos shows this color form venturing from their normal rocky habitat. In the intermediate area between rocks and grass where there is just sand, spotted or striped fishes seem to be more at ease. The golden barb in the lower right hand photograph is perfectly colored. Note the huge deposit of fish excretion on the bottom. This disintegrates into a fine mulm amongst which the barbs like to poke.

when they swim above the rocks they swim in a normal position. When they swim alongside the rocks they swim with their bellies parallel to the rocky surface and when they are underneath the rocks they swim upside down. Is it any wonder that most mbunas and even *Pelvicachromis* spawn upside down inside flowerpots? This probably derives from their habit of spawning in dark caves underneath a rock. More evidence for my anti-egg spot theory.

On these facing pages are four different color varieties of *Pseudotropheus zebra* though all would be placed into the BB morph. BB, by the way, stands for "black bar." The W morph indicates "white"; the B morph are "blue" and the OB morph is "orange blotched".

Note on these facing pages that the lighter the fish the lighter the habitat in which it is found. Note how well the egg spots stand out in the darker areas.

This *Pseudotropheus microstoma* (or *Ps. tropheops micro-stoma* as some people would have it) had more black than any of the "zebra-striped" morphs I ever saw. This specimen was in some 35 feet of water. Note all the fish excreta on the rock.

Labeotropheus trewavasae, above; below, *Haplochromis tetrastigma*, which is found in shallow water where it finds the bottom epiphytes upon which it feeds.

These two photos, above and below, were taken within a few feet of each other and show the typical assortment of fishes found on the rocks (mbuna) and those which venture out onto the sand. Malawian fishes have a definite preference for habitats and fish collectors know in advance what species of fishes can be found in any particular habitat.

4
How Cichlids feed

Cichlids have been successful in the African lakes because they have found ways to feed on practically every living resource in their range. They have developed specialized teeth and mouth structures, and they even have developed specialized internal organs with which to utilize special foods.

Many *Tilapia*, for example, feed on microscopic plants and animalcules which are collectively referred to as phytoplankton. Herring and menhaden are similar feeders, and like certain *Tilapia* (but by no means ALL *Tilapia*) they cannot be caught

Fishes such as *Labeotropheus* with mouths located on the underside of their bodies feed upon the algae in an almost horizontal position to the strata upon which they are feeding.

In 12 feet of water where the rocky meets the grassy, sandy habitat the fishes enjoy ample food supplies. Different genera feed at different angles due to the formation of their mouths and jaws.

This photo was taken in 4 feet of water where the *aufwuchs* is very thick due to the increased amount of light falling upon the surface of the rocks.

on hook and line. Basically, phytoplanktonic feeders merely suck in food on a continuous basis, filtering out those particles which are edible and ingesting them. They have special gill filaments which assist in the filtering process. In captivity it is possible to feed these fishes the usual aquarium fare, for many of them also have teeth.

Many phytoplankton feeders also feed from the bottom on sediment, thus emphasizing the fact that their teeth might have some ancillary use. I was quite amazed at the numbers of *Tilapia* which followed the hippos, awaiting their bowel movements to rush at the droppings in a frenzy. Mbunas rarely peck at bottom sediment, and it was quite interesting to note the huge amount of droppings accumulated on the flat stones and sandy bottoms near the mbuna sites. So thick was the sediment near mbuna sites that the water was stirred to a muddy cloud by the action of my flippers when I swam by. This was extremely annoying, as it made picture-taking very difficult; I had to remove my flippers to take successful photographs in such areas.

This is a smooth rock which has been covered with *auf-wuchs,* the algae upon which the entire mbuna population is dependent for food.

This photograph clearly shows the different angles that fishes use to attack the *aufwuchs* (algae). This photo was taken in 12 feet of water near Cape McClear, Lake Malawi.

On the sandy bottom of Lake Malawi the fishes seem to have a 45° angle of attack. They grab mouthfuls of sand, sift it through their gills, and remove those bits of nutrition which are available.

The mbunas are what the Germans call *aufwuchs* feeders. The name *aufwuchs*, which literally means "luxuriant growth", is applied to the half-inch thick covering of slimy algae which covers the rocks' surfaces in which the mbunas are found. *Pseudotropheus tropheops* and all its many morphs are found feeding solely on such algal growth; the fish's 8 rows of small teeth assist it to scrape off mouthfuls of this high protein food. In the aquarium they usually adapt to eating almost anything, partly accounting for their success as an aquarium fish, but if you really want to see them at work, put in a piece of lettuce or spinach and watch them go to work reducing it to a few fine strands. *P. zebra* and *P. fuscus,* even though they have quite different dentition, also feed on this same aufwuchs, as do the *Tropheus* of Lake Tanganyika.

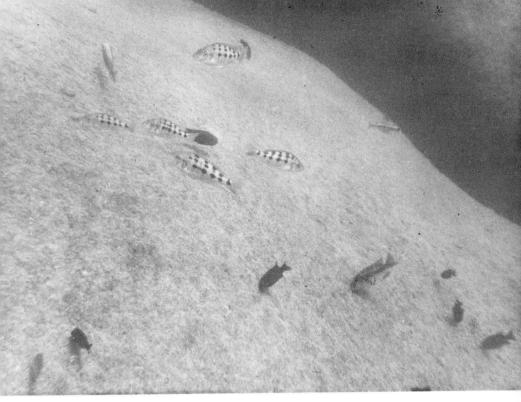

The *aufwuchs* found on the Lake Malawi rocks (upper photo) is quite different from that found in Lake Tanganyika (below). Note the sponges (green in natural color) in the Tanganyikan habitat.

Petrotilapia tridentiger from Lake Malawi.

Petrochromis fasciolatus from Lake Tanganyika.

Tilapia rendalli from Lake Tanganyika.

Lethrinops furcicauda from Lake Malaw

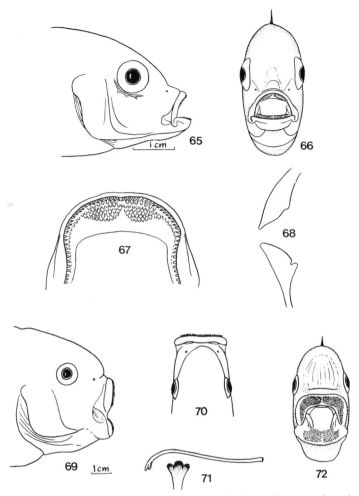

Heads, jaws and teeth of a scraper of rocks and leaves, and a rock-scraper, from L. Malawi. 65–68—*Cyathochromis obliquidens*: 65—Head, lateral; 66—Head, anterior; 67—Upper dentition; 68—Opposing outer teeth of upper and lower jaws. 69–72—*Petrotilapia tridentiger*: 69—Head, lateral; 70—Head, dorsal; 71—Single tooth seen from the side, with detail of its expanded tip in face view; 72—Head, anterior

The sketches and caption above were taken from Fryer and Iles' *"The Cichlid Fishes of the Great Lakes of Africa."*

One Malawian cichlid, *Petrotilapia tridentiger,* has spoon-shaped teeth and a flexible mouth that fits to the irregular shape of the rock surface, enabling the fish to very efficiently remove the aufwuchs. In the Chitonga language of Malawi, these fish are called *"mbuna kumwa,"* which means "rock hitter," referring to the way these fish "attack" a rock. The *Petrochromis* species from Tanganyika are remarkably similar in habit. It is fairly easy, by the way, to identify certain genera of cichlids from a distance just by watching their feeding habits. *Petrotilapia* and *Petro-*

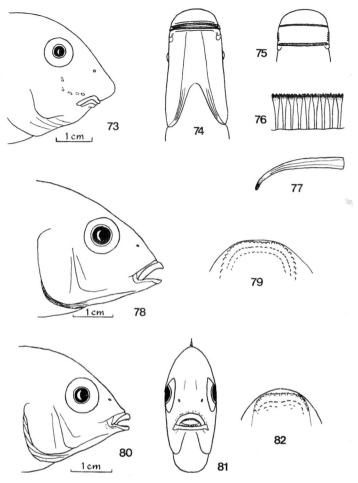

Heads, jaws and teeth of an algal-eating rock scraper, a specialist picker of algal filaments, and a general *Aufwuchs* eater all from L. Malawi; 73–77—*Labeotropheus fuelleborni*: 73—Head, lateral; 74—Heads, ventral; 75—Jaws, semi-ventral, with mouth open; 76—Anterior row of teeth, anterior; 77—Single tooth from this row, lateral. 78–79—*Haplochromis guentheri*: 78—Head, lateral; 79—Upper dentition. 80–82—*H. fenestratus*: 80—Head, lateral; 81—Head, anterior; 82—Upper dentition

The sketches and caption above were taken from Fryer and Iles' *"The Cichlid Fishes of the Great Lakes of Africa."*

chromis usually attack a rocky surface perpendicular to it. *Pseudotropheus* species are found at a 45° angle when feeding, while *Labeotropheus* species are almost parallel to the rocky surface when they feed, facilitated of course by their ventral mouths.

Amongst the algal growths are to be found many small copepods, but since the fish usually scrape away the algae and "inhale" what they scraped away while preparing for the next scrape, they give the free-swimming copepods a chance to swim away from the mild stream flowing into the fish's mouth, so a careful observation

Head study of *Haplochromis mloto.*

Head study of *Haplochromis placodon*.

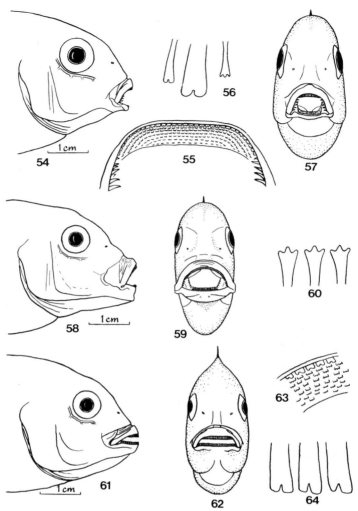

Heads, jaws and teeth of three algal-eating rock scrapers from
L. Malawi. 54–57—*Pseudotropheus tropheops*: 54—Head, lateral; 55—Dentition
of upper jaw; 56—Details of bicuspid and tricuspid teeth of upper jaw; 57—
Head, anterior. 58–60—*P. zebra*; 58—Head, lateral; 59—Head, anterior; 60—
Arrangement of tricuspid teeth of posterior rows. 61–64—*P. fuscus:* 61—Head,
lateral; 62—Head anterior; 63—Arrangement of teeth in upper jaw; 64—Teeth
of outer row of upper jaw

The sketches and caption above were taken from Fryer and
Iles' *"The Cichlid Fishes of the Great Lakes of Africa."*

of the fish feeding shows only a scattering of small copepods. In
the aquarium all the known species (known to aquarists, that is)
readily adapt to feeding on the usual aquarium diet. They do
especially well on prepared foods and while living foods are
accepted, they do not seem to suffer from a lack of living foods
the way South American cichlids do.

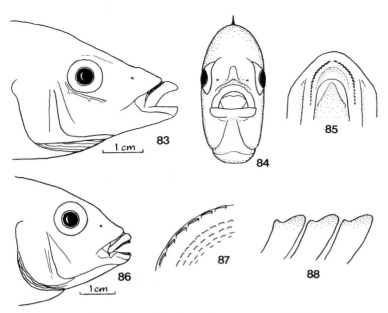

Heads, jaws and teeth of a plant scraper and a leaf chopper from L. Malawi. 83–85—*Hemitilapia oxyrhynchus*: 83—Head, lateral; 84—Head, anterior; 85—Upper dentition. 86–88—*Haplochromis similis*: 86—Head, lateral; 87—Part of upper dentition; 88—Outer teeth of upper jaw, lateral

Some cichlids, notably *Haplochromis similis, Tilapia rendalli* and *T. zillii,* prefer leafy plants. While their diet presumably depends upon water plants, they graze on any leaf, and the African fishermen take advantage of this fact. Several fishermen I observed dumped sweet potatoes, yams and casava leaves into an easily seined area and left the deposit there for a few hours before they seined the area to catch the fishes which were feeding upon the leaves. I examined the stomach contents of several of these fishes and found them filled with these heavy leaves.

Some of the larger species of cichlids, such as *Chilotilapia* of Lake Malawi, *Macropleurodus* of Lake Victoria, and *Haplochromis sauvagei,* eat snails and mussels. Some of these fishes merely crush the snails, many of which are two inches in diameter, while others merely grasp the extended foot and shake the body out of the shell.

The usual feeding habits of many fishes depend upon eating other fishes or aquatic and terrestrial insects and crustaceans. *Lethrinops furcifer* from Lake Malawi, for example, is found only on sandy stretches near the shore, and its sole diet seems to be small worm-like larvae found in the sand. The fish merely dives headfirst into the sand, gathering a mouthful of sand which it passes through its gill rakers, filtering out the small larvae. A fish

Many Malawian cichlids dig into the sand, scoop up a mouthful and pass it over the gill raker sieves to remove food particles. The sketches show successive positions of *Lethrinops furcifer* and two types of gill rakers. The shape of the gill rakers is very important in the classification of fishes. The photograph was taken by H. Hansen in the Berlin Aquarium. The sketches are from Fryer and Iles' *"The Cichlid Fishes of the Great Lakes of Africa."*

This fish was caught in fairly deep water. It represents a new genus and species, *Cleithrochromis bowleyi* from Lake Malawi; it was recently described by Mr. Eccles. The "Mae West" appearance might well serve to protect the fish from digging too deeply into the bottom (see sketch on facing page).

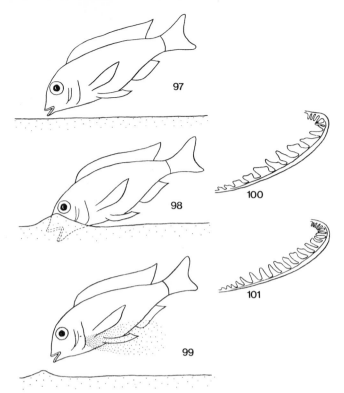

Diggers in sand from L. Malawi. 97–99—Successive positions as *Lethrinops furcifer* fills its mouth with sand and passes collected material through its gill raker sieve; 100—Outermost row of gill rakers; 101—Outermost row of gill rakers. *Lethrinops* sp. (Note the difference in spacing of the gill rakers, which is associated with selection of different foods by these closely related species.)

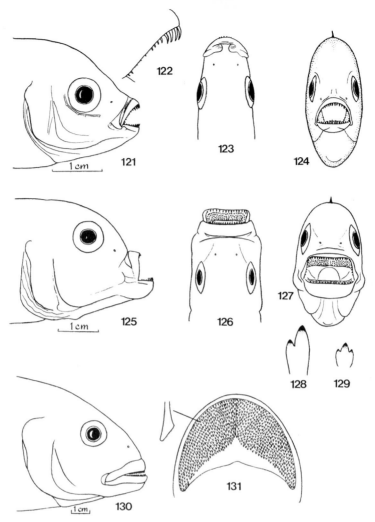

A zooplankton feeder and two scale eaters from L. Malawi.
121–124—*Cynotilapia afra*: 121—Head, lateral; 122—Teeth of upper jaw; 123
—Head, dorsal; 124—Head, anterior. 125–129—*Genyochromis mento*: 125—
Head, lateral; 126—Head, dorsal; 127—Head, anterior; 128—Outer tooth of
lower jaw; 129—Inner tooth of lower jaw. 130–131—*Corematodus shiranus*:
130—Head, lateral; 131—Upper dentition.

The sketches and caption above were taken from Fryer and
Iles' *"The Cichlid Fishes of the Great Lakes of Africa."*

I collected in open waters with a seine, a new genus and species
probably, has a sort of shield on its chest which might very well
protect it from being buried in the sand when it may be diving
for such mouthfuls of sand. This is merely speculation on my
part, as I did not observe the fish feeding. *Lethrinops* would
probably do best in the aquarium when fed *Tubifex* worms.

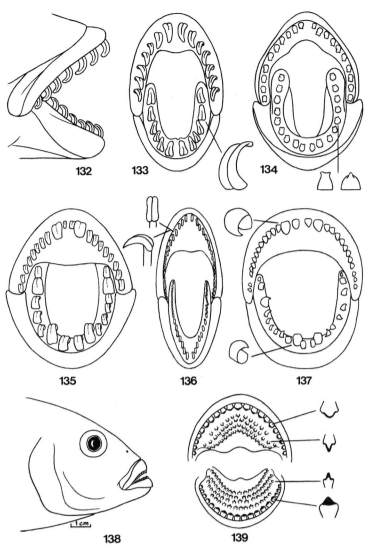

132   133   134

135   136   137

138   139

The scale eaters of L. Tanganyika and a fin biter from L. Malawi. 132 and 133—*Plecodus paradoxus.* 134—*Perissodus microlepis.* 135—*Plecodus straeleni.* 136—*Plecodus multidentatus.* 137—*Plecodus elaviae.* All show the jaws either laterally or from in front. 138 and 139—*Docimodus johnstoni:* 138—Head, lateral; 139—Dentition of the jaws. Redrawn after Boulenger and Poll.

The zooplankton feeders are fishes which feed upon the minute crustaceans living in the water. They all have protrusible jaws and have earned the name *"utaka,"* which seems to defy translation. They would do very well in the aquarium on a diet of *Daphnia* or brine shrimp, as crustaceans seem to be their preferred diet.

Haplochromis livingstonii, head study.

Haplochromis lepturus, head study.

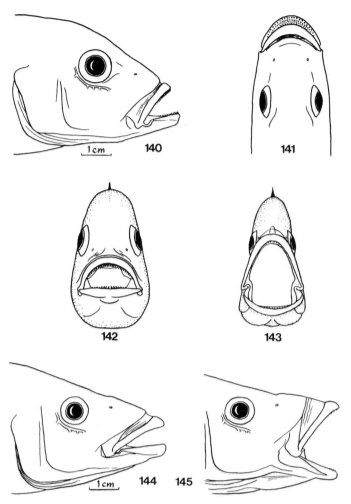

Piscivores from L. Malawi. 140–142—*Haplochromis pardalis*: 140—Head, lateral; 141—Head, dorsal; 142—Head, anterior. 143–145—*H. Polyodon*: 143—Head, anterior; 144—Head, lateral; 145—Head, lateral, with mouth open

The sketches and caption above were taken from Fryer and Iles' *"The Cichlid Fishes of the Great Lakes of Africa."*

In Lakes Tanganyika, Malawi and Victoria are to be found fishes which eat scales. Even South America has a piranha-like fish, *Catoprion mento*, which also is a scale eater. *Plecodus* and *Perissodus* species from Tanganyika eat scales, as does a *Haplochromis*, two species of *Corematodus* and *Genyochromis mento*. It is very interesting that almost all of these fishes have different dentition, indicating that their evolution was dissimilar.

86

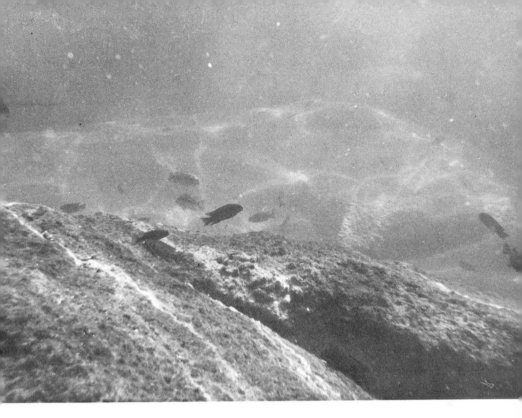

Rocks and sand as they appear in Lake Malawi (upper photo) and Lake Tanganyika (lower photograph.)

Lethrinops gossei, female, head study.

Haplochromis mloto, head study.

Of the scale eaters, the *Corematodus* species are the fishes of most concern to aquarists, because they do not eat large scales like their homologous species, but prefer the small scales found on the tails of such small fishes as the mbunas. One of my first observations while diving among the mbuna was that they almost all had had chunks taken out of their tails.

In the aquarium the scale eaters seem to only eat scales! I do not know of any case where any scale eater, including *Catoprion mento,* lived for an extended period of time (say six months) unless it had fish scales in its diet! It is doubtful that the scale eaters restrict themselves to scales, as I have seen them remove fins (or at least parts of fins, especially the tail) in their attempts to remove scales.

In Lake Malawi there is a very interesting fish known as *Haplochromis compressiceps.* What makes this fish so special is that it attacks the eyes of fishes. I observed three *Haplochromis compressiceps* feeding and they attacked small fishes by aiming at their eyes and swallowing the whole fish. I saw two instances in which they attacked a fish almost twice their size and left an empty eye socket as a result of their attacks. They appear to

Catoprion mento is the South American scale-eater which resembles a piranha. The Germans call it the "Wimple Piranha" or the "Flag Piranha."

A closeup of the head and jaws of *Catoprion mento* from South America.

attack anything shining in the water, and hard-shelled insects were fed upon as well.

There are many other feeding specialists. Some rob eggs from nests, while some steal fry swimming about the nests. There are reports that certain fishes grasp brooding fishes by the mouth, forcing them to release their mouthful of eggs or fry into the mouth of the attacking fish. I have been unable to personally verify this feeding behavior.

To summarize, you should observe your African cichlids and attempt to ascertain their food of choice. It is rare (except for scale eaters) that a fish will eat only one food. In their range fishes probably specialize because they rarely leave the immediate neighborhood of their "home" and thus do not have the opportunity of a selective diet. Basically, mbunas are vegetarians while utakas prefer crustaceans, but I have seen mbunas rise to the surface of an aquarium as a flying insect hits the water, and I have also observed utakas eating a piece of lettuce.

91

Haplochromis pholidophorus, head study.

Haplochromis nitidus, head study.

5
How Cichlids Breed

The various kinds of mouths and teeth of African cichlids seem to have nothing to do with their breeding habits, even though African cichlids utilize their mouths in one way or another for breeding.

Those cichlids which lay their eggs on a flat, hard surface, usually use their mouths and teeth to scrub the surface clean before they lay their adhesive eggs. These eggs are then guarded and fanned until they hatch. Other species, and this pertains particularly to those species of cichlids found in Lakes Malawi and Tanganyika, are mouthbrooders. Especially in the Malawian endemic forms, the eggs, once laid and fertilized by the male, are gathered in the mouth of the mother fish and kept there until they hatch. Even after hatching, the young still flock to the mother's mouth for protection and safe harboring while they are growing.

Very few African fishes depend upon the father for buccal protection; the mother seems to be the one who cares the most! This characteristic is by no means peculiar to African cichlids. Many South American cichlids, a few anabantoids, and such truly ancient fishes as *Osteoglossum* (the aruana or arowana) also practice mouthbrooding.

Because of the physical problems involved in carrying first the eggs and then the young in their mouths, the size of the spawn of mouthbrooding cichlids is necessarily limited. Several scientists have counted the ripe eggs inside the body of dead fishes they collected. Often these eggs numbered thousands (a 10-inch *Tilapia aureum* had 4300 eggs; a 22-inch specimen of *Tilapia nilotica* had 3706), but never have this many eggs been found in any fish's mouth. In *Tilapia esculenta,* for example, as many as 1600 eggs have been found in ripened ovaries, but no one was ever able to find more than 711 eggs in any female's mouth.

The name *Tilapia mossambica* was recently changed to *Saro-therodon mossambicus* by Dr. E. Trewavas. It is a mouth-brooder in which both parents will care for the eggs and young, although it is almost always the females that take over the chores. The only species placed in the genus *Tilapia* are nest brooders; those in *Sarotherodon* are mouthbrooders.

Tilapia are quite different from mbuna. The *Tilapia* are, as a rule, hardier and more adaptable. They seem to thrive wherever they are introduced providing enough food is available and the water is sufficiently warm. For this reason we find *Tilapia* introduced into every continent in the world where rice is grown. Certainly, if you have *Tilapia,* you should be warned against releasing them into your local waters. It doesn't take too much for them to become established and crowd out native species. *Tilapia* are prohibited in many areas because of this problem.

Mbuna, on the other hand, would quickly perish without exactly perfect circumstances. They must have rocks and they must have soft, thick algae growing on those rocks. The brood size of most mbunas is probably well under 75 (Fryer claims that 50 eggs is probably the maximum), and often the ovaries of various mbuna contain but a few dozen ripened eggs. There is a record of 17 eggs in a ripe *Pseudotropheus zebra* ovary; a *Labeotropheus trewavasae* had only 10 eggs in her mouth; *Tropehus moorii* carries between 5 and 10 eggs to incubate, while *Tropheus duboisi* laid a

Melanochromis auratus eggs three days old. Photo by Dr. D. Terver, Nancy Aquarium, Nancy, France.

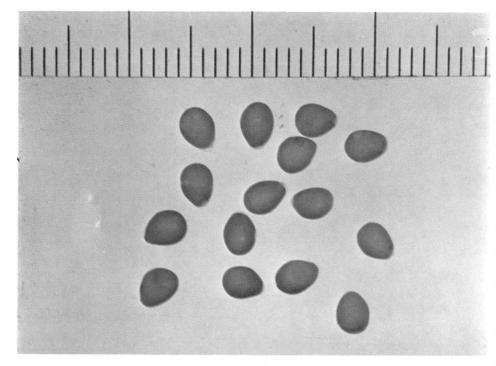

Julidochromis ornatus in a typical habitat. Note that one fish is guarding its niche against a possible intruder. Photo by Hansen, Berlin Aquarium.

mere 10 eggs during an observed spawning. Is it any wonder tank-raised African mbunas are more expensive than the larger, wild-caught fishes?

Examinations of mbunas have produced evidence that only one ovary produces eggs, usually only the right ovary. Many *Haplochromis* have atrophied (smaller) right ovaries, especially in Lake Malawi, so it is possible that nature is protecting itself from over-population in Lake Malawi by limiting the number of eggs produced by cutting in half the number of ovaries producing eggs! That certainly could help the human overpopulation problem. Wouldn't it be nice if women produced eggs from only one ovary . . . every two months . . . cutting birthrates substantially?

The eggs of many African mouthbrooders are colorful. While most are eggyolk yellow, many have red in them, with the red changing the basic yellow color to orange, brown or tan. The eggs are fairly dense, usually with less than 60% water, and they are almost uniformly fairly large.

While diving in Lakes Malawi and Tanganyika, but especially in Lake Malawi, I was constantly amazed at the number and variety of nests to be observed in shallow water (under 30 feet deep) where there was sand. All of the nests were round and crater-like, but some were truncated cones and one was built on a huge, flat rock, the sand obviously having been carried from a distance by the male who was, at the time I observed the nest, guarding the site and moving off 10 to 20 feet at a time in all directions searching for a mate . . . or two.

I have observed at least five species spawning in Lake Malawi and several in Lake Tanganyika. Because I did not collect the fish it would be difficult to say exactly which species they were, but I will generalize about their spawning activities because they were all almost identical.

Using their nests as a base of operations, the males would swim inside large areas which seem to be bounded by an imaginary circle with a radius of ten feet from the center of the nest. They almost always moved in straight lines to the circumference of the circle to meet a fish who appeared to slowly approach the nest site. When the fish was of a different species . . . or another male of the same species . . . the nesting male would attack the fish sharply, driving it off. I never saw an intruding fish fight back: they always left the area quickly, even though they might have been larger than the nesting male. As the nesting male approached and noticed that the intruder was a female of the same species, he

A pair of *Sarotherodon mossambicus.* The male is the lower fish. In the photo below, a male *S. mossambicus* shows the lips characteristic of an older fish. Top photo by Milan Chvojka; lower photo by Gerhard Marcuse.

Cyathopharynx furcifer (in the center of the photograph) digging its nest in about 20 feet of water in Lake Tanganyika.

In the aquarium *Julidochromis ornatus* look for a secure, dark place in which to lay their eggs. Photo by Hans Joachim Richter, Leipzig, DDR.

would immediately perform his ritual dance, spreading his fins to their fullest and showing clearly the markings in his tail, dorsal and anal fins. He would continue the dance for a minute or two, then swim back to his nest waiting for the female to follow. In most cases the female did not immediately follow the male, but would remain in the area just outside the imaginary boundary of the spawning area. The male, after waiting for a minute or two, would then swim back out to the female and try the same tactics all over again. This would be repeated, sometimes for hours, until finally the female came into the nesting arena, or she left.

Once the female arrives on the scene, the male invites her right onto his nest, and the female cautiously investigates. Her symbol of acceptance of the male seems to be her mouthing the nest herself. She then joins the male near the center of the nest. At this time the male seems to make passes on the center of the nest,

As the pair of *Sarotherodon mossambicus* prepare to spawn, they dig a deep hole in the sand.

As soon as the male fertilizes the eggs, the female takes them into her mouth. Note how this photograph compares in the position of the fishes with the egg-spot proof of Dr. Wickler on page 32 . . . and these males have no egg spots!

The male *Sarotherodon mossambicus.* Note the distended mouth pouch. Photo by Gerhard Marcuse.

With fully extended fins, the male invites the female *Julido-chromis ornatus* to join him under the rock he has selected as a spawning site.

The female *Julidochromis ornatus* joins the male and together they prepare the spawning site.

A male *Sarotherodon mossambicus* with fry. The fry are feeding on the microorganisms which are present on the algae-covered log. Photo by Gerhard Marcuse.

possibly laying down a stream of sperm. His action is almost exactly like those of male South American cichlids as they fertilize a chain of eggs previously laid by a female. After a short swim with his vent very close to the bottom of the nest, the male is joined by the female in a swim of increasingly tighter circles. Finally, in a circle so tight that the tail of one is almost in the mouth of the other, the pair snuggle next to one another and the eggs are laid amidst a substantial amount of quivering by both fish. All during the ceremony, the male proudly displays his anal fin eggspots; the female always seems to be impressed with them, even attacking them at times. Wickler suggests that during these attacks, she is able to get sperm to fertilize her mouthful of eggs, but probably it is merely a recognition sign which helps the fish distinguish one species from the other. Immediately after spawn-

The female *Sarotherodon mossambicus* signals her fry with a wriggle of her body, and they swiftly return to the refuge of her mouth. Photo by Gerhard Marcuse.

As the male watches, the female *Julidochromis ornatus* lays two eggs (not visible).

The male *J. ornatus* quickly comes and fertilizes the pair of eggs laid by the female.

A male *Sarotherodon mossambicus* shows his distinctive white chin while guarding his free-swimming fry. The male of this species rarely takes part in the care of eggs or fry but may do so if they are neglected by the female. Photo by Gerhard Marcuse.

In *Tilapia macrochir,* the female mouths the genital tassel of the male. Her mouth is swollen with eggs. The thin string is a sperm thread and will facilitate fertilization of the eggs in the female's buccal cavity. Photo from Fryer and Iles' *"The Cichlid Fishes of the Great Lakes of Africa."*

ing, the female takes the eggs into her mouth and moves off the nesting site.

Typical of masculine behavior, once the female leaves the nesting site, the male immediately looks for another female. I saw one male spawn with three females within a 40-minute period. This same behavior might be observed in an aquarium, but it would have to be a fairly large one.

Another surprise characteristic of certain African cichlids is the elongated pelvic fins of *Ophthalmotilapia* and *Ophthalmochromis,* which are colored on the ends. Certain species of *Tilapia,* on the other hand, have special tassels hanging from the genital pore of the male and, during spawning, the female mouths them, assumedly getting confused between eggs and tassels and getting additional sperm in her mouth during the process.

When the female lays her eggs, they must be fertilized almost immediately, for a few moments later is too late. Though the time varies between species and water condition (pH, temperature,

Spawning continues for *J. ornatus* over a period of about an hour with about 35 eggs being laid.

The eggs are guarded by the female and fanned as they
slowly develop. Photos in this series by Hans Joachim Richter, Leipzig, DDR.

As the thousand or so fry grow, they become more and more difficult to handle and they flee to both parents' mouths when danger threatens. The male and the female equally share this burden, though the female seems more willing.

Its almost impossible to believe that these three photos (see facing page and above) were taken within ten seconds of each other!!! The male actually has all of these baby fish in his buccal cavity . . . and I don't think he swallowed one of them.

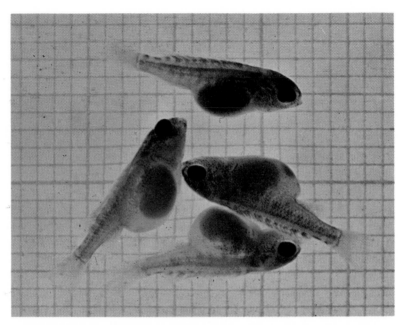

The fry above were taken from the buccal cavity of a female *Melanochromis auratus* a few days after the eggs hatched. The lower photograph shows the fry a few days later, having absorbed their yolk and just about ready to look for their own food. Photos by Gerhard Marcuse.

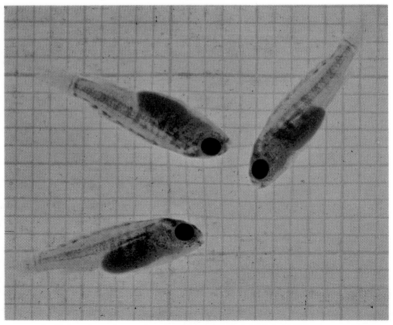

This wonderful photograph by A.F. Orsini shows a female *Melanochromis auratus* releasing her young to feed. The young resemble miniature adult females, the males attaining their own pattern at maturity.

hardness, etc.), it can be generalized that eggs not fertilized within the first five minutes of being laid will never get fertilized. The reason for this is that the egg case begins to harden almost as soon as it hits the water. Once it becomes too hard the sperm are unable to penetrate the egg surface and thus the egg cannot be fertilized. This has important consequences in the acceptance or rejection of various theories of fertilization . . . for one must not be hasty in accepting the egg tassel theory (or the eggspot theory) . . . the physical properties giving rise to the theories might very well be recognition symbols . . . and this author believes they are nothing more than that!

Once the female (and in a few cases, the male) picks up the fertilized eggs, their incubation begins. Sometimes, if she happens to be an mbuna from Lake Malawi, she'll carry her eggs and young for three weeks, or even a month; other times, when the female might be a *Tropheus* from Tanganyika Lake, the poor female might be stuck with her eggs and fry for almost two

The female *Sarotherodon* accepting her fry.

months (56 days seems to be the record for a *Tropheus duboisi*). During this period the females do feed, regardless of what certain books say to the contrary. Some *Tilapia,* which brood for less than 3 weeks (19 days is about the average), however, can live without feeding, but they might feed while the fry are out of their mouths during the last week of their brooding period.

It has been very difficult to raise mouthbrooder eggs without a parent. The main reason for this is that the eggs are so heavy that the development within the egg is in a small area, the balance of the egg being utilized for food storage. If the eggs are not tumbled about and "chewed" during their storage in the mouthbrooder's buccal cavity, the yolk settles in the bottom of the egg, disturbing the development of the germinal disc and killing the developing embryo. A theoretical substitute for the mouthbrooder's cavity might be a 2 inch-diameter plastic tube through which air is bubbled to gently agitate the eggs on a continuous basis.

6
Breeding African Cichlids in the Aquarium

It is obvious that large areas in which huge nests can be built is practically impossible for the average home aquarium, yet so adaptable are the *Tilapia* and related genera of African fishes, including *Haplochromis*, that spawning them in aquaria is possible. The ability of the author to generalize about a "perfect spawning" aquarium is necessarily limited. It would be much safer to research in the various books on breeding aquarium fishes, or in hobbyist magazines where individual species are discussed, and attempt to lay out an aquarium suitable to fulfill the needs of the fish in question.

This is a typical rock outcrop in Lake Malawi. The rocks continue under the water in about the same configuration. This would be the ideal setup model for an aquarium, except in miniature of course.

Albino *Pseudotropheus zebra* do not exist in nature. Photo by Ken Miner.

Pelvicachromis pulcher spawning in a flowerpot upside down. This is typical of many African cichlids being a carry-over from spawning under large rocks in their normal range. Photo by Hans Joachim Richter, Leipzig, DDR.

For those fishes which build a sand nest, it would be advisable to have an aquarium with 4 inches or more of coarse sand on the bottom of the tank. A few rocks and submerged logs would probably be helpful, as would a large plant growing from a fairly heavy flowerpot. Needless to say, the larger the aquarium, the better. Certainly the aquarium should be at least 6 times as long and 4 times as wide as the length of the fish.

For mbunas and other rock dwellers, it would be advisable to have as many rocks and hiding places as possible, again with a deep base of coarse gravel. The mbunas will probably dig a pit under a rock and proceed with their spawning ritual as secretly as possible.

For the African cichlids which lay their eggs out in the open, or some of the 'Pelmatochromis' species of the Congo River system, large flat rocks would be advantageous.

A typical rocky bottom in Lake Malawi. The depth is about 35 feet.

A sandy, grassy habitat in Lake Malawi. Find the fish!

The majority of African cichlids are territorial. They stoutly defend their own territories even in their native habitat. Of course the territorial boundaries are basically imaginary, but let a newcomer to the aquarium dive into another fish's sanctuary and there likely will be serious trouble. For this reason, large aquaria are necessary, and crowding must be kept to a minimum. The only safe technique for introducing fishes to an already established aquarium in which there are many long-time residents is to move all the rocks and hiding places into new positions so all can have an equal chance to re-establish their territories.

Most African cichlids fight and bite each other, especially when males become breeding-conscious. You must watch your fishes closely and remove those fishes which seem to be getting the abuse. Once a fish becomes a loser, its demise cannot be far away, for fish lore is absolutely correct in its stress on "survival of the fittest." Most wise pet shop owners keep their African cichlids in tanks in which they have no place to hide. This allows for a better display of the fishes offered for sale and prevents territorialization. Unfortunately this type of accommodation

This series shows '*Pelmatochromis*' *thomasi* laying their eggs.   Photos by Hans Joachim Richter, Leipzig, DDR.

124

African cichlids are not the only mouthbrooders. This cichlid comes from Paraguay and is known as *Geophagus balzanii*. Note the mouthful she has! Photo by Hans Joachim Richter, Leipzig, DDR.

keeps the cichlids in their least favorable coloration, but at least they are relatively safe from sexual and territorial competition.

If it is possible, pairs of mbunas and rock dwellers should be isolated in tanks with dimensions of at least 12 × 12 × 30 inches, though the author has used aquaria of 100 gallons in which six spawning pairs successfully found their own territories and were able to raise half a dozen babies on a fairly regular basis.

In outdoor pools in Florida, mbunas and Tanganyikan rock dwellers did very well. For one thing they rid the pool of tadpoles and crawfish. How they did this the author was unable to ascertain, but in pool after pool the tadpoles and crayfish gradually disappeared. A close examination of the pools, however, indicated that the mbunas, not having rocks, dug very deep caves, perhaps two feet deep, into the sides of the mud/clay banks. They successfully spawned and raised small quantities of fry, but as soon as the water temperature in the pools dropped below 68°, the mbunas had problems and gradually died. Perhaps they became the victims of snakes or water turtles as their metabolism slowed down?

Thirty feet depth in Lake Tanganyika. Lots of rocks, murky water and not much light or algae.

7

Diseases of African Cichlids

African cichlids are relatively hardy fishes, as are most cichlids. They are susceptible to almost all the diseases of aquarium fishes, including but not limited to white spot disease (ichthyophthiriasis), slime bacterial infections which aquarists refer to as mouth fungus or tail or fin rot, and some fairly sophisticated diseases related to whirling disease (*Myxosoma*). In the thousands of mbuna that I observed and collected, almost every fish, most especially the smaller ones, were parasitized by the larval stages of several digenetic trematodes. It seems the metacercarial stage, one of the early stages in the development of the parasite, bores its way into the skin of the fish and forms a black cyst. In light-colored fishes the cysts are very obvious, while in darker fishes they are hardly noticeable. The cysts do not seem to aggravate the fishes; in tests the author made, the parasites required an intermediate host in order to reinfect other fishes in the same aquarium. It is quite possible that the fish itself is only one vector in the life history of the parasite, and in order for the encysted parasite to progress to the next stage in its life it must pass through the digestive tract of a fish-eating bird (of which there is no scarcity in the great lakes of Africa).

As a general rule, all African cichlids collected in their native ranges have black cysts and torn fins, but they quickly recover their full finnage if kept in situations which are non-competitive, usually within a week. The black cysts sometimes eventually disappear, as the cysts may well be expelled from the fish the way any foreign imbedment would be dislodged by the natural forces in most vertebrate animals. Thus African fishes with black spots are not to be considered as "diseased" though they certainly do harbor parasites.

White spots, bloody ulcers or open wounds are quite another story. These signs can only mean problems, and the most immediate attention should be paid to clearing up the condition as quickly as possible. There are many books on the diseases of fishes and it is almost unthinkable that any aquarist wouldn't have a few fish disease books in his library . . . they are probably the best investment one can make as far as the aquarium hobby is concerned.

A new species of *Pseudotropheus* from Lake Malawi. The new species in this book will be described in *Tropical Fish Hobbyist* magazine as soon as their characteristics have been thoroughly studied.

Haplochromis taeniolatus, head study of breeding male. Note the parasites in the pectoral fin.

8
Identifying African Cichlids

The classification of African cichlids, like the classification of all other fishes, is a highly specialized skill. The ichthyologists to whom fish classification is a specialty are known as taxonomists. They usually work in large public institutions and have developed fields of interest. It would be rare, for example, for an ichthyologist studying marine fishes also to undertake the study of a group of freshwater fishes, and it would be equally rare for a scientist studying cichlids to care to get involved in catfishes.

Lake Tanganyika. The fish in the foreground are *Lamprologus brichardi*; the single fish is *Julidochromis marlieri*.

African cichlids have a dozen or so working ichthyologists prying into their secrets. For the most part, the study of African cichlids has been centered in England, Belgium and Germany. Dr. Max Poll, the great Belgian ichthyologist, has spent a whole lifetime working on the fishes of the Congo, including a very thorough study of the fishes of Lake Tanganyika. Fryer, Eccles, Jackson and others have done extensive work on Lake Malawi. Essentially their work is concentrated in a few scientific books, mostly without any color photographs and without any photographs of living fishes. These scientists, for the most part, depend upon the characteristics of dead, preserved fishes upon which to make their determinations. They can, however, usually make a good guess about which fish is which from a good photograph, and should you have an identification problem, it would be best to send the photo to one of the recognized authorities in the field or check one of the more highly illustrated books.

Without a preserved specimen *positive* identification is almost impossible for any scientist.

For the purpose of this book, the author has selected a large variety of photographs to assist the beginner in identifying the most common fishes of Lakes Malawi and Tanganyika, with a few of the other popular African cichlids added for comparison. For a greater insight into understanding African cichlids there are two excellent texts which are readily available at every pet shop which specializes in fishes, or even at your local library. These books are:

The Cichlid Fishes of the Great Lakes of Africa by Dr. Geoffrey Fryer and T. D. Iles, and *Cichlids of the World* by Dr. Robert Goldstein. The Fryer and Iles book is a very scientific book, extremely well written, but poorly illustrated. The Goldstein effort is extremely well illustrated but not as scientifically detailed, though this by no means reduces its value for the non-scientist. Fryer and Iles is intended for scientists . . . Goldstein is intended for hobbyists. Both make excellent reading and are highly recommended.

Pseudocrenilabrus philander(?) spawning in an aquarium. The female is picking up the eggs just as the male fertilizes them. Photo by Ruda Zukal.

The female *Pseudocrenilabrus philander*(?) with her buccal cavity bulging with eggs. Photo by Ruda Zukal.

9
Cichlids of Lake Malawi and Surrounding Waters

The following list of fishes has been taken freely from the CHECK LIST OF THE FISHES OF NYASALAND. The check list was prepared by P. B. N. Jackson and issued as *National Museums of Southern Rhodesia* Occasional Paper 25B, Causeway, Southern Rhodesia, 1961. Since the issuance of this report there have been additional fishes discovered and described from the lake, but no attempt has been made by the author to bring the list up to date, for even at the time of this writing the author has on his desk at least 11 new species and one new genus awaiting description in a suitable journal.

GENUS *TILAPIA*

Tilapia sparrmani A. Smith. Not found in Lake Malawi but present in Lake Chilwa and the Banga River. It also ranges to the Limpopo, Zambesi and Congo and is the most widely distributed species of the genus in Africa (other species have been introduced worldwide artificially.) Called *bream* in Malawi. An omnivorous feeder.

Tilapia melanopleura A. Dumeril. One of the few fish found in the lake as well as in surrounding waters. This fish has been successfully introduced worldwide for fishfarming purposes. Eats plants and hides in thick beds of *Ceratophyllum*. Called the *red-breasted bream.*

Tilapia shirana Boulenger. Found only in Lake Malawi. Has fine scales on the caudal fin as do all Malawi cichlids except

T. sparrmani, T. melanopleura, Haplochromis callipterus
and *H. moffati* (now known as *H. philander*). Differs from
other Lake Malawi *Tilapia* by having four anal spines
while others have three. Closely related to *T. mossambica*
of the Zambesi. Eats plants and detritus. Does very well
in pond culture. Suggested popular name *spiny bream.*

Tilapia squamipinnis (Guenther) is the best food fish in Lake
Malawi. It is called "chambo", and about 6,000,000 pounds
of the fish are landed each year. This is a mouthbrooding,
pelagic species which eats plankton and other microscopic
foods.

Tilapia saka Lowe is a close relative of *T. squamipinnis* and can
hardly be differentiated from this fish. Lowe claims the
fish differs from *squamipinnis* because it has different
breeding and feeding ranges. Also called "chambo" by
Lake Malawi fishermen.

Tilapia lidole Trewavas is another popular food fish and is also
called "chambo" by Lake Malawi fishermen.

Tilapia karongae Trewavas is closely related to *squamipinnis, saka*
and *lidole* but has a smaller head, and the toothed area of
the pharyngeal bone is straight and not concave. A rare
species found only in the northern end of Lake Malawi.

GENUS *HAPLOCHROMIS*

Haplochromis philander (Weber), previously known as *H. moffati.*
A humorous error made by Jackson: "*Haplochromis
philander* . . . named after Dr. Robert Moffat, a famous
South African missionary." This is a very widespread
species.

Haplochromis callipterus (Guenther). Common species. Adults eat
snails.

Haplochromis maculimanus Regan. Known only from the type,
190 mm. in total length.

Haplochromis livingstonii (Guenther). A very colorful fish, carnivorous in habit; it is associated with underwater beds
of *Vallisneria* and is only found where this common plant
is plentiful. The fish seems to be more common on the
eastern than the western shores of Lake Malawi. Some
juveniles from the mouth of a brooding female from
Likoma Island lived in an aquarium for some time and the
tiny fishes showed exactly the same well marked blotches
as the adults. The name "kaligono," meaning "the
sleeper," is given to this fish on account of its habit of

Haplochromis livingstonii.

Haplochromis decorus.

Haplochromis callipterus. The upper photo shows a close-up of the unpaired fins. Photos by Michael Oliver in Monkey Bay, Lake Malawi.

lying flat on the bottom and shamming death, presumably until some unsuspecting little fish comes within striking distance. Named for Dr. Livingstone. Known to 20 cm. in length.

Haplochromis pardalis Trewavas . From Deep Bay near the north end of the lake, also found among rocks in Nkata Bay. Carnivorous. The type is 19 cm. long.

Haplochromis polystigma Regan . A brown-mottled (hence its Chinyanja name "hyaena" and Chitonga name "leopard"), rock-frequenting species, caught by angling with fish bait on a small hook, and by small-meshed gill-nets set over rocky places. Known to 23 cm. in length.

Haplochromis venustus Boulenger . A sand-frequenting carnivorous species, probably also inhabiting *Vallisneria* beds. A specimen from Bana had fish bones in its stomach. Breeding males a most beautiful peacock blue with a sulphur-yellow blaze down the nose. Largest known size, 22.5 cm.

Haplochromis fuscotaeniatus Regan . Not seen by the J.F.R.O. survey, apparently occurs mainly in the south end of the lake. British Museum specimens are 14–22 cm. in length.

Haplochromis fenestratus Trewavas . Common over rocky shores where, although showing relatively few specializations, it is one of the very few successful non-predatory species of *Haplochromis*. An omnivorous feeder on the fauna and flora of rock surfaces. Largest known size, 12.7 cm.

Haplochromis johnstoni (Guenther). An abundant and distinctive little fish very characteristic of the sandy shores of the main lake. Associated with *Vallisneria* to such an extent that, at Nkata Bay, both the fish and the plant bear the same native name! A female with young has been seen to deposit her brood onto the *Vallisneria,* swim round and protect them, and take them up into her mouth again. Named for Sir Harry Johnston, and known to 17 cm. in length.

Haplochromis longimanus Trewavas . Forty specimens, the longest 14.5 cm., collected by Christy from the south end of the lake, are in the British Museum. Not otherwise known.

Haplochromis micrentodon Regan . Known only from the south end of the lake. Largest recorded length 15 cm.

Haplochromis moorii (Boulenger). A blue-colored species distinctive by virtue of its possessing a large frontal hump above and between the eyes. A bottom dweller mainly of sandy areas. Has been observed skulking round other fishes such as *H. rostratus,* digging in the sand, and snatching food in the disturbed sand and mud. Grows to at least 20 cm. Named for Prof. J. E. S. Moore.

Haplochromis subocularis (Guenther). A sheltered-water, sand-dwelling species apparently restricted to the south end of the lake. Largest known size 16 cm.

Haplochromis ornatus Regan . A rock-frequenting species which feeds on the insect nymphs and larvae which occur on and under rocks. Not very common, grows to about 20 cm. The lips may be produced into small lobes, reminiscent of *H. euchilus.*

Haplochromis lobochilus Trewavas . Described from one specimen (Christy collection) from Deep Bay, 100 mm. in total length. Not otherwise known.

Haplochromis ericotaenia Regan . Closely related to the preceding three species; there are sixty-four specimens in the British Museum, but there are no data on its habits. Largest known size 20 cm.

Haplochromis tetrastigman 'Guenther . A fish commoner in the south, where it is sometimes of commercial importance, being seined occasionally in large numbers. Probably a bottom feeder on sandy shores, and grows to 15–16 cm. Very close to the genus *Lethrinops.*

Haplochromis heterodon Trewavas . The males of this species, although usually only 13–17 cm. in length, build a circular nest in the sand which has a diameter of about 50 cm. and is raised up 15–20 cm. above the ground on which it is built.

Haplochromis placodon Regan . A well marked, easily recognized species common on sandy bottoms and *Vallisneria* beds all over the lake. Feeds on molluscs and has heavy pharyngeal dentition to crush the shells. Grows to about 25 cm.

Haplochromis decorus Trewavas . Six specimens, 10.8–16.5 in total length, collected by Christy, but there are no further data.

Haplochromis argyrosoma Regan . Not abundant, over rocks and open water at both ends of the lake. A British Museum specimen measures 14.5 cm.

Haplochromis stonemani.

Haplochromis   macrostoma   (?).

Haplochromis argyrosoma.

Haplochromis nitidus.

Haplochromis selenurus Regan . A midwater species, not abundant and more common in the south. Largest known size 16.5 cm.

Haplochromis rostratus (Boulenger). This well marked fish is one of the lake cichlids most commonly seen. Like certain sea fishes its long snout is used for burrowing in the sand over which it lives. Able to bury itself in the sand to escape seine nets.

Haplochromis maculiceps Ahl . Only two specimens known, the largest 29.5 cm. from the north lake.

Haplochromis macrostoma Regan . A heavily built predator probably more common at the south end of the lake, though known from the north and often caught in small-mesh gill-nets.

Haplochromis polyodon Trewavas . Not uncommon at Nkata Bay over rocky shores, where it is one of the most important piscivorous species and grows to about 30 cm. in total length.

Haplochromis urotaenia Regan . Largest known size 22 cm.

Haplochromis spilopterus Trewavas . Rarely seen during the J.F.R.O. survey, caught off Kota Kota in $2\frac{1}{2}$ in. gill-nets over a sandy bottom. A predator on other fishes. Largest recorded size 20 cm.

Haplochromis rhoadesii (Boulenger). A predatory fish of the southern lake whose habits are not yet known. A British Museum specimen measures 33 cm. Named for Comdr. E. C. Rhoades, R.N.

Haplochromis gracilis Trewavas . Described from three specimens collected by Christy, the largest 21 cm. in length. Not otherwise known.

Haplochromis spilostichus Trewavas . Described from a single specimen from Monkey Bay, 22 cm. in total length; not otherwise known.

Haplochromis ahli Trewavas . There are nineteen specimens in the British Museum (Christy collection) from both ends of the lake, the largest 16 cm. in total length; there are no other data. Named for Dr. E. Ahl of Berlin.

Haplochromis pleurospilus Trewavas . Described from one specimen collected by Christy from a sand bank in the northern lake, 53 mm. long. Not otherwise known.

Haplochromis auromarginatus (Boulenger). A handsome little cichlid which feeds off bottom epiphytes in shallow water.

142

Has been seined, gill-netted and occasionally taken in chirimila nets from Fort Johnston to Nkata Bay and Likoma. The largest is 24 cm. (British Museum).

Haplochromis ovatus Trewavas . A very handsome blue fish, often with bronze yellow streaks down the nose, which floats about in midwater near the shore. Often seen from ships at anchor. Grows to about 20 cm.

Haplochromis pholidophorus Trewavas . Described from a single specimen from Vua, 10.5 cm. long. Not otherwise known.

Haplochromis woodi Regan . A well known, easily recognized and widely distributed predatory species, caught in seines, gill-nets and by angling. Largest known size about 25 cm. Named for the naturalist and collector R. C. Wood, Esq.

Haplochromis modestus (Guenther). A species of doubtful validity, only the type, 15 cm. in total length, being known.

Haplochromis tetraspilus Trewavas . A small fish apparently common in the southern lake, but nothing seems known of its habits. Largest recorded size 15.6 cm. (Christy collection).

Haplochromis chrysogaster Trewavas . Known only from three specimens, one from Karonga and two from the southeast arm, the largest being 175 mm. in total length.

Haplochromis labifer Trewavas . A member of the bottom-feeding sandy beach fauna, often caught in seine-nets operated in bays. The largest known is 21.7 cm. in total length.

Haplochromis speciosus Trewavas . Possibly a fish of the southern lake only, as it is described from two specimens from Vua and Monkey Bay, the largest 24.5 cm. long; there are no other published records.

Haplochromis nitidus Trewavas . Described from eleven specimens collected by Christy from both ends of the lake, the largest 13.9 cm. in total length, but not otherwise known.

Haplochromis pictus Trewavas . Described from eight specimens collected by Christy from both ends of the lake, the largest 12.6 cm. in total length, but not otherwise known.

Haplochromis intermedius (Guenther). A fish of the southern lake, but there is no information on it. Probably a plankton eater, and grows to over 21 cm.

Haplochromis compressiceps (Boulenger). A fish easily recognizable by its very thin face as well as by its color pattern. Predatory on other fish, intermediate between rock and sand. Not abundant, grows to over 23 cm.

Haplochromis subocularis. The eye has been discolored by the preservative (formalin) in which the fish was placed prematurely. Below is a closeup of the head (note the teeth) of the same fish.

Haplochromis anaphyrmus.

Haplochromis euchilus Trewavas . A very striking fish, both in its color pattern and the way its lips are produced into large lobes. Fairly common but not abundant, associated with a rocky habitat. Grows to at least 22 cm. in length.

Haplochromis epichorialis Trewavas . Nothing is known about the habits of this fish. Two from Deep Bay in the Christy collection, 20 cm. long.

Haplochromis balteatus Trewavas . Described from three specimens from Karonga and Vua (Christy collection). Largest known size 9 cm.

Haplochromis melanotaenia Regan . An uncommon species frequenting sandy shores and *Vallisneria* patches. Seems to occur mainly in the south in Monkey Bay. Nothing is known of its feeding habits. Largest recorded length 18 cm.

Haplochromis sphaerodon Regan . A third species closely related to *balteatus* and *melanotaenia* but differs in having a smaller head. Habits probably similar. Largest known 11.5 cm.

Haplochromis lateristriga Guenther . Taken in seine-net at Palm Beach, south-east arm. Feeding habits unknown. Not common. Largest known size 19.5 cm.

Haplochromis incola Trewavas . A species with heavy pharyngeal teeth from *Vallisneria* beds. Probably a mollusc eater, mostly from the south. Length to 19.5 cm.

Haplochromis mola Trewavas . Closely related to the preceding species but more abundant in the north. Not uncommonly taken in seine-nets off sandy beaches, Nkata Bay. A mollusc eater, grows to about 18 cm.

Haplochromis plagiotaenia Regan . A fish of sandy shores and calm sheltered waters, more common in the south. Grows to 11 cm.

Haplochromis labidodon Trewavas . Described from five specimens from Mwaya and Deep Bay (Christy collection), not otherwise known. Largest known size 18 cm.

Haplochromis festivus Trewavas . Known only from the type, one specimen collected by Christy in the British Museum from Nkudzi, 88 mm. in total length.

Haplochromis pleurotaenia Boulenger . This species, collected from Lake Malawi by J. E. S. Moore, was wrongly labelled as being from Lake Tanganyika by him, the mistake being discovered by Trewavas places *H. microstoma* Regan in the synonomy of this species. Occasionally taken in

146

seine-nets from deeper water with a sandy bottom. Grows to about 20 cm.

Haplochromis phenochilus Trewavas . A well marked fish; the pallor of the lips is very striking. J.F.R.O. took specimens from Mwafufu near Nkata Bay, from the intermediate zone. Said occasionally to be caught in large numbers by seine-net in the south-east arm and is then of fair economic importance. Grows to about 20 cm.

Haplochromis kirkii (Guenther). A common and abundant little fish with heavy pharyngeal bones from sandy shores and sheltered waters. Insect and mollusc remains have been found in the stomach. Named for Sir John Kirk. A British specimen measures 18 cm.; usually smaller.

Haplochromis labridens Trewavas . Closely related to the preceding species but not as abundant and occurring mainly in the south end of the lake. Largest known size 16.5 cm.

Haplochromis virgatus Trewavas . Also closely related to *H. kirkii;* the J.F.R.O. survey took one specimen (14 cm.) in a small-meshed gill-net over rocks at Nkata Bay.

Haplochromis holotaenia Regan . A predatory fish, seldom seen but taken near rocks over sand and *Vallisneria* interspersed with rocks. A predatory species, grows to over 20 cm.

Haplochromis kiwinge Ahl . A well known and important species. Adults are largely, but not entirely, predators on other fish and frequently are caught by anglers on spoons and with bait. Breeding males are frequently caught by spinners trolled over their nests; they rise up and attack the spinners, usually getting foul-hooked. Caught also in seines and gill-nets. This is a valuable food and sporting fish, growing to about 30 cm. Breeding males are a beautiful blue with each scale flecked by a golden spot.

Haplochromis strigatus Regan . An easily recognized mildly predatory fish from sand and *Vallisneria* patches. Eats insects; tiny fish and vegetable remains have also been found in stomach. A British museum specimen measures 22.3 cm.

Haplochromis dimidiatus (Guenther). A moderately large predatory species associated with sandy bottoms, where it is omnivorous but largely carnivorous, feeding on invertebrates and fish. Known up to 26.5 cm. in length.

Haplochromis orthognathus Trewavas . One specimen from Nkata Bay taken by J.F.R.O. Four from the Christy

Haplochromis pholidophorus.

Haplochromis nigritaeniatus.

Haplochromis annectens.

Haplochromis eucinostomus.

collection were taken in rather deep water in the south-west arm of the lake. The vertical mouth and thick lips are very striking. Probably inhabits intermediate rock/sand zone. A Christy specimen measures 19.5 cm.

Haplochromis melanonotus Regan. More common in the south, the dentition of this fish suggests a specialized feeding habit, but it is not known what it is. Probably frequents sandy beaches. Known to grow to 24 cm.

Haplochromis semipalatus Trewavas. Described from four specimens from Deep Bay and Kapora (Christy collection), the largest 18.5 cm. in length, but otherwise unknown.

Haplochromis guentheri Regan. A rock-frequenting species with specialized dentition. Picks certain algae from rock surfaces, and often shows a high degree of selectivity in feeding. Known from both ends of the lake, largest known size 20 cm. Named for the late Dr. A. Guenther of the British Museum.

Haplochromis mollis Trewavas. A rare sand-frequenting species of the south lake. One taken by J.F.R.O. off sand at Palm Beach, south-east arm. Largest known size 16 cm.

Haplochromis spilorhynchus Regan. A well known large *Haplochromis*, predatory upon other species, especially from the south-east arm and Upper Shire. Fairly valuable as food. Grows to 26 cm. or more.

Haplochromis caeruleus Boulenger. Closely related and of similar habits to the preceding, but is probably of a more mid-water habitat, having been caught by J.F.R.O. more frequently in gill- than in seine-nets.

Haplochromis formosus Trewavas. A rare species occasionally found off rocks. About 12.5 cm. is the largest known.

Haplochromis spectabilis Trewavas. Described from eight specimens (Christy collection) to 25 cm., but not seen since. If a valid species, will be predatory and fish eating.

Haplochromis obtusus Trewavas. Described from one specimen from the southern lake, measuring 22 cm. in total length, but not seen since.

Haplochromis lepturus Regan. A common large *Haplochromis* predatory on other fish, characteristic of the sandy beaches of the open lake. A good angling fish and often taken in seine-nets. Not common in the south, more often found from Kota Kota northwards, 40 cm. in length.

Haplochromis atritaeniatus Regan . A predatory fish-eating species of the southern lake and Upper Shire, possibly associated with weed. Largest known size 24 cm.

Haplochromis oculatus Trewavas . A predatory, fish-eating species, closely related to *Haplochromis nototaenia* and its allies, from the south lake. A British Museum specimen measures 26 cm. in length.

Haplochromis nototaenia (Boulenger). Another large predatory member of the species-flock. Lives over sand in sheltered waters and takes the place of the preceding species in the south. Common and well known; grows to about 40 cm.

Haplochromis heterotaenia Trewavas . A very large fish-eating *Haplochromis* that penetrates to all depths to the limit of dissolved oxygen, and was found to be an important food fish when fished for by deep-set gill-nets. Commoner in the northern part of the lake. Grows to over 40 cm. in length.

Haplochromis triaenodon Trewavas . Twenty-six specimens, from 65 to 145 mm. in total length, in the British Museum from the Christy collection, all from the south end of the lake.

Haplochromis similis Regan . A very common and abundant little fish, found in estuaries and river mouths as well as in the main lake. A vegetarian, feeding by chopping bits off submerged vegetation such as *Vallisneria*. Largest recorded size, 17 cm.

Haplochromis marginatus Trewavas . Another common little cichlid of sheltered sandy-bottomed waters, hence more abundant in the south and at places such as Kota Kota. Trewavas (1935) has recognized two subspecies, one from the north and one from the south end of the lake. Superficially very similar to *H. similis* but actually a quite distinct species, with teeth of jaws and pharynx smaller and pharyngeal bones more slender. Maximum size about 16 cm., but usually smaller.

Haplochromis leuciscus Regan . Little is known about this fish which is not common but probably also a calm-water sand-frequenting species. Largest known size 14.5 cm.

Haplochromis spilonotus Trewavas . A rare cichlid with a longitudinal stripe. Two in British Museum (Christy collection) and J.F.R.O. has a record from Nkata Bay. Largest known size 16.5 cm.

Haplochromis chrysonotus.

Haplochromis longimanus.

Haplochromis venustus, female above; male in photo below.

Haplochromis insignis Trewavas . Not seen during the survey. Five specimens from Monkey Bay collected by Christy, the largest 19.6 cm.

Haplochromis annectens Regan . A handsome blue fish, not common, found usually in midwater close to shore a few feet off the bottom. Grows to over 20 cm. in length.

Haplochromis taeniolatus Trewavas . Uncommon, occasionally taken in seine-nets from deepish water over sand. Largest known size 11.3 cm.

Haplochromis breviceps Regan . Not seen by the J.F.R.O. survey; probably very local in distribution. Only four, the largest 15 cm., are known, all in the British Museum.

Haplochromis microcephalus Trewavas . There is no data on this fish of which only two specimens (collected by Christy) are known from Monkey Bay, the largest 12.5 cm. in length.

Haplochromis nigritaeniatus Trewavas . Nine specimens (the largest 20.4 cm.) in British Museum from Monkey Bay (Christy collection), but not otherwise known.

Haplochromis serenus Trewavas . A handsome blue fish living in midwater off the bottom. Grows to 25 cm.

Haplochromis purpurans Trewavas . Not seen by either the J.F.R.O. or the 1939 survey. Fifteen specimens (Christy collection) from the north end of the lake, the largest 17.5 cm.

Haplochromis eucinostomus Regan . Mainly shoaling, plankton-eating, and of great economic importance, mainly in the northern lake. A sand-loving fish, which also builds nests on sand. Taken in small numbers by seine and chirimila (open-water seine) over suitable habitats. Largest known size 12.5 cm.

Haplochromis inornatus (Boulenger). Known only from the two types, 8.5 and 9.5 cm., never seen since. If a valid species, probably associated with sand of very limited occurrence.

Haplochromis flavimanus Iles . A sand-loving species, almost a "border-line utaka," as its feeding habits are closely associated with the substrate. Sporadic in occurrence, caught for instance in chirimilas in March near "chirundus" (under-water rock formations), otherwise not abundant. Zooplankton feeder, but generally found with sand grains, phytoplankton, filamentous algae, etc., in stomach as well. Grows to 12 cm. in total length.

Haplochromis mloto Iles . Found occasionally in association with *H. virginalis*, but probably prefers a more sandy habitat and has sometimes been taken in beach seines. Also found far out in the lake and perhaps the most pelagic of the utaka. Superficially similar to *H. eucinostomus* but is easily distinguished by having more gill-rakers. Grows to 13.5 cm. in total length.

Haplochromis virginalis Iles . Common, even abundant in places, can be caught all the year round near rocks. One of a complex, perhaps two species involved. Feeds entirely on zooplankton and has a short breeding season from March to June. Largest known size 13.2 cm.

Haplochromis prostoma Trewavas . Six specimens in British Museum from Vua and Deep Bay, and twenty-three specimens taken all on the same occasion at Nkata Bay. Has the protrusible snout pointing definitely downward, possibly connected with a bottom, sand-frequenting habit. Probably rather rare, largest known size 11.5 cm. in total length.

Haplochromis boadzulu Iles . A remarkably local species, found only at White Rock and Boadzulu Island, south-east arm, but in a typical "chirundu" rocky habitat, which is very uncommon in this part of the lake. Largest known size 10.9 cm.

Haplochromis cyaneus Trewavas . An "utaka" species from the south end of the lake. There is one in the British Museum of a total length of 19 cm.

Haplochromis trimaculatus Iles . Very similar to the next species from which, apart from color, it differs in having a longer pectoral fin, a shorter preorbital, a different head profile, a slightly larger eye, and a longer and slightly shallower caudal peduncle. Widespread and fairly common in rocky habitats. A borderline member of the "utaka" group, with a less protractile mouth, but a plankton feeder and found with other members of the group in typical "utaka" habitats. In young stages shoals near the "chirundus" (underwater rock formations); when older and larger tends to be more solitary, and then caught occasionally inshore in $2\frac{1}{2}$ in. and 3 in. gill-nets. The African name, meaning replete or distended, refers to the large stomach always crammed with zooplankton and often *Botryococcus*.

Haplochromis kiwinge.

Haplochromis labridens.

Haplochromis taeniolatus.

Haplochromis jacksoni.

Haplochromis pleurostigma Trewavas . In rocky habitats, only moderately common. Like *Haplochromis trimaculatus* not a typical "utaka", and has a shorter protractile mouth than the others. Grows to over 20 cm. in total length.

Haplochromis chrysonotus (Boulenger). A fish of widespread distribution, found as far apart as Monkey Bay and Karonga. Prefers open water, congregates round floating objects such as logs and boats at anchor. Rare, caught at "chirundus" (underwater rock formations). One in the British Museum measures 16.3 cm. in total length. Insects, algae and bottom detritus is taken, as well as zooplankton

Haplochromis nkatae Iles . Closely related to, but less common than, the above, occasionally caught at "chirundus." Largest known length 14.5 cm. A ripe female taken from a sandy beach in August.

Haplochromis jacksoni Iles . Appears occasionally near "chirundus" in shoals, and large adults are taken in gill-nets off rocky shores. Similar in general appearance to *Haplochromis chrysonotus* but with more spines and rays in dorsal fin, as well as other differences. Breeding fishes have been recorded in March. Largest known size 18.3 cm. Named for P. B. N. Jackson, Esq. officer-in-charge of the J.F.R.O. Malawi survey.

Haplochromis borleyi Iles . Moderately widespread, relatively inshore in rocky habitats, found near deep "chirundus," usually in small numbers. Seems to have a wider range of habitat among the rocky shores than other "utaka." Male in breeding dress is especially brilliantly colored and smaller than the female. Largest known size 12.9 cm. Named for H. J. H. Borley, Esq., at one time Director of Game Fish and Tsetse Control, Malawi.

Haplochromis pleurostigmoides Iles . Apparently localized in distribution. At Nkata Bay more common near "chirundus." Does not apparently occur at Likoma Island. Largest known size 14.8 cm.

Haplochromis quadrimaculatus Regan . Widespread over the lake, the most abundant "utaka" and the most important economic species. Fished during the breeding season, the peak being May, June and July. Caught by chirimilas at chirundus, also by small-mesh gill-nets on rocky shores. Young remain inshore until 110–120 mm., caught very near rocks. Adults rarely caught outside breeding season;

some of them probably range out into the open lake, further than any other species of "utaka."

Haplochromis likomae Iles . Recorded only from Likoma Island where it is the subject of a large fishery. Closely related to *Haplochromis quadrimaculatus*, but is not as abundant as this species. Largest known size 14 cm.

GENUS *LETHRINOPS*

Fishes of this genus are difficult to differentiate and have not yet been extensively studied, so that little is known of their habits and ecology. No species of *Lethrinops* is known to occur off rocks; some, e.g. *L. praeorbitalis*, are found in deep water off a sandy bottom, and most are to be found off sandy shores, often associated with *Vallisneria* beds, various species exhibiting some zonation in depth. All are, so far as is known, carnivorous, but none are predatory. Food includes crustaceans and other fauna of *Vallisneria* beds, chironomid larvae and molluscs. Work on the micro-habitats of these fishes, half a dozen species of which are frequently pulled up in a single haul of the seine-net, would make a most interesting study. The group is in desperate need of revision, and at least two new species await description. The species described in Jackson, et al, are listed in full, but some names are probably synonymous.

Lethrinops variabilis Trewavas . Appears to be more abundant in the south, and recorded to 17.3 cm. in total length.

Lethrinops liturus Trewavas . Forty-seven specimens in the British Museum to 16.8 cm.

Lethrinops brevis (Boulenger). A small and one of the more abundant species. Digs chironomid larvae out of the sand of sandy beaches. Largest recorded size 16.3 cm.

Lethrinops trilineata Trewavas . Described from a single specimen of 13.2 cm.

Lethrinops microstoma Trewavas . Only known from twenty Christy specimens in the British Museum, to 14.5 cm.

Lethrinops parvidens Trewavas . Quite common in the south-east arm. Largest recorded size 12.8 cm.

Lethrinops intermedia Trewavas . This species has the middle posterior teeth of the pharyngeal enlarged and blunt. Known only from six specimens from the southern lake. To 16 cm.

Haplochromis atritaeniatus.

Haplochromis chrysonotus.

Haplochromis boadzulu.
Hapiochromis virginalis.

Lethrinops cyrtonotus Trewavas . Described from a single specimen, 11.2 cm.

Lethrinops macrophtalmus (Boulenger). Known only from four young fish, to 8 cm., the types of *Tilapia macrophthalma.*

Lethrinops aurita (Regan). Described from the type of *H. auritus,* 8 cm. (Wood collection), the types of *H. macrochir,* 11.5 and 13 cm. (Wood Collection), and twenty-one specimens 93–140 mm. (Christy collection).

Lethrinops longimanus Trewavas . Described from a single specimen, 13.3 cm. (Christy collection).

Lethrinops macracanthus Trewavas . Described from a single specimen, 20 cm. (Christy collection).

Lethrinops alta Trewavas . Described from a single specimen, 15.8 cm. (Christy collection).

Lethrinops argentea Ahl . Known only from four types in the Berlin museum, to 17.5 cm.

Lethrinops lethrinus (Guenther). First collected by Johnston. Commoner in the south. Grows to over 20 cm.

Lethrinops leptodon Regan . Closely related to *Lethrinops lethrinus* and recorded to the same length.

Lethrinops lunaris Trewavas . Known only from British Museum specimens, to 18.6 cm.

Lethrinops oculata Trewavas . Known only from a single specimen, 13.5 cm. (Christy collection).

Lethrinops alba Regan . The type, 10 mm. in total length, was collected by Johnston. Twenty-three Christy specimens measure 10.5–16.5 cm.

Lethrinops furcifer Trewavas . A common species on sandy shores, at least in the northern part of the lake. It has evolved a specialized feeding mechanism which enables it to collect the chironomid larvae which occur buried in the sand on such beaches. Largest recorded size (collected by Christy) 19.5 cm., but usually smaller.

Lethrinops furcicauda Trewavas . Known only from nineteen specimens (Christy collection), to 21 cm.

Lethrinops christyi Trewavas . Known only from three specimens to 18.3 cm. and named for the collector.

Lethrinops laticeps Trewavas . One of the largest species, closely related to and doubtfully distinct from *Lethrinops praeorbitalis.* Largest recorded size 30 cm.

Lethrinops praeorbitalis (Regan). The largest species of the genus and of fair economic importance in some areas. Penetrates fairly deep down, taken in large numbers in 40 meters of water off Monkey Bay and the southern lake. Caught in large seine-nets off Kota Kota in fair numbers. Feeds on the bottom, largely on *Chaeoborus* larvae. Grows to over 30 cm. in length.

GENUS *HEMITILAPIA*

Hemitilapia oxyrhynchus (Boulenger). Very close to *Haplochromis* but has characteristic jaws and teeth. Inhabits the zone intermediate between rock and sand, where it browses among *Vallisneria* beds, scraping the algae and insects (*aufwuchs*) from their leaves. Grows to about 20 cm., but usually smaller.

GENUS *RHAMPHOCHROMIS*

A group of silvery, elongate cichlids, predatory on other fishes, with large heads, and jaws with spaced conical teeth. Have an open-water or pelagic existence, and some species penetrate down to the limits of dissolved oxygen. Occasionally form shoals and are a valuable economic and sporting group, caught in gill-nets, by hand lines, and on silver spinners or fish bait, fresh "usipa" being the best of the latter. Most species are closely related and the group is in need of revision. The lengths given are the greatest total length recorded by Trewavas, in each case for British Museum specimens.

Rhamphochromis longiceps (Guenther). Length 25 cm.
Rhamphochromis macrophthalums Regan . Length 27 cm.
Rhamphochromis brevis Trewavas . Length 40 cm.
Rhamphochromis lucius Ahl . Length 36 cm.
Rhamphochromis woodi Regan . Length 42 cm. Named for the
    naturalist and collector, Mr. Rodney Wood.
Rhamphochromis ferox Regan . Length 43 cm.
Rhamphochromis esox (Boulenger). Length 37 cm.
Rhamphochromis leptosoma Regan . Length 38 cm.

GENUS *TREMATOCRANUS*

Trematocranus auditor Trewavas . Known only from three specimens (2 Rhoades, 1 Christy), from Vua and 9.6 cm. in length.
Trematocranus brevirostris Trewavas . Known only from two specimens (Christy collection), the longest 7.2 cm. in total length, from the south end of the lake.

163

Hemitilapia oxyrhynchus, with plant found in its range.

Trematocranus microstoma Trewavas . Known only from twenty specimens (Christy collection), the largest 23.2 cm. in total length, mainly from the northern lake.

GENUS *AULONOCARA*

Aulonocara machochir Trewavas . Known only from one specimen 17 cm. long, collected by Christy.

Aulonocara nyassae Regan . An insect-eating species living where rocky and sandy shores merge. Probably widespread but as the optimum conditions for its existence are of relatively rare occurrence it is never very abundant. Maximum known length 18 cm.

Aulonocara rostrata Trewavas . Twenty-seven specimens (Christy collection) up to 18 cm. in length, but not otherwise known.

GENUS *LICHNOCHROMIS*

Lichnochromis acuticeps Trewavas . Rare, apart from the type in the British Museum there is only one specimen, taken in a gill-net off rocks during the J.F.R.O. survey.

GENUS *DIPLOTAXODON*

Diplotaxodon argenteus Trewavas . A distinctive, rather uncommon species with a large eye, usually found in open and deepish water. Predatory on other fishes, it is usually taken by gill-net, but a number of very small juveniles were taken in a seine-net near the Ruhuhu River in February, 1955. There may be more than one species in this genus.

GENUS *ARISTOCHROMIS*

Aristochromis christyi Trewavas . A handsome fish from the vicinity of rocks in deepish water, mainly in the northern part of the lake. A predator on other fishes. Like most Lake Malawi cichlids the male has a beautiful blue breeding dress. Named for the collector and explorer, Dr. Cuthbert Christy.

GENUS *SERRANOCHROMIS*

Serranochromis robustus (Guenther). The only species of its widespread genus in the area, and a well-known sporting fish. Predatory on other fishes, it is especially abundant at Ft. Johnston, but also occurs in the lower reaches of rivers and off rocks in the open lake. Grows to about 50 cm. in length.

GENUS *CYNOTILAPIA*

Fishes of this and the following eight genera are known as the 'Mbuna' group, this being the collective name for this assemblage of small, mainly rock-frequenting species. Most are closely related and show beautiful adaptations to their methods of feeding.

Cynotilapia afra (Gunther).

GENUS *LABEOTROPHEUS*

Labeotropheus fuelleborni Ahl . A very common species on rocky shores where it obtains its livelihood by scraping algae from rocks by means of its remarkable straight tooth-lined jaws. Like *Pseudotropheus zebra* it exhibits polymorphism; there being two very distinct colour forms among the females. Grows to 11 cm. in size. Named for Dr Fuelleborn, a Germany army surgeon.

Labeotropheus trewavasae Fryer . Extremely closely related to the foregoing and like it exhibiting colour polymorphism. Longest recorded size 11.7 cm. Named for Dr E. Trewavas of the British Museum.

GENUS *PETROTILAPIA*

Petrotilapia tridentiger Trewavas . A very handsome fish whose coloration is very variable. By attaining a length of about 25 cm. it can probably claim to be the largest of the 'Mbuna'. Common and widespread on rocky shores, and penetrates to the limits of dissolved oxygen, occasionally caught in deep-set gillnets at over 200 feet depth. Feeds on loose algae.

GENUS *GEPHYROCHROMIS*

A genus closely related to *Pseudotropheus* but is not so strictly rock-frequenting.

Gephyrochromis moorii Boulenger . Originally erroneously recorded from Lake Tanganyika (coll. Moore), there are little data for this species, but it probably lives on sandy bottoms, dredging diatoms from the substrate. The type of *C. nyasana* measured 11.4 cm. in total length, and the type of *G. moorii* 12 cm.

Gephyrochromis lawsi Fryer . This species appears to prefer coarse shingle and boulders to a true rocky habitat. Browses on algae. Largest recorded size 12.8 cm. Named for the Methodist missionary Dr Robert Laws.

GENUS *CYATHOCHROMIS*

Cyathochromis obliquidens Trewavas . A species of areas where rocky and sandy shores merge. Here it is often the most abundant fish, yet it seldom ventures among rocks and seldom or never on to true sandy beaches. Trewavas records its length as up to 15 cm.

GENUS *PSEUDOTROPHEUS*

Pseudotropheus minutus Fryer . As its name implies this is a very small fish, being in fact in all probability the smallest cichlid found in Lake Nyasa. Not uncommon in shallow water on rock shores. Largest recorded size 6.3 cm.

Pseudotropheus lucerna Trewavas . Differs from other members of the genus by having its habitat intermediate between the rocky and sandy shores, thus often picking up sand grains among its algal food. Largest recorded size 13.5 cm. (Christy collection.)

Pseudotropheus williamsi (Gunther). A species readily recognizable by the presence of two horizontal series of spots on the flanks. Not one of the commonest of the 'Mbuna'. Largest size known 16.5 cm. Named for the collector Mr C. Williams.

Pseudotropheus elegans Trewavas . Only one specimen known, from Deep Bay, collected by Christy, and 11 cm. long.

Pseudotropheus livingstonii (Boulenger). Fryer's recent work produced only four specimens of this species. All these came from rather deeper water than that frequented by most of its relatives. Closely related to *P. zebra*. Largest size known 15 cm. (Christy collection.) Named for Dr Livingstone, the famous explorer.

Pseudotropheus zebra (Boulenger). No fewer than four very distinctive colour forms of this species occur in the lake, and although their relative abundance varies from place to place, all four co-exist in some localities. One of the commonest species on rocky shores where it subsists on algae scraped from rock surfaces. Largest known size 11 cm.

Pseudotropheus elongatus Fryer . Known only from a few specimens, but these came from both east and west sides of the lake. Like most members of its genus it is an algal browser. Largest recorded size 8.2 cm.

Triglachromis otostigma, young male above; *Limnochromis auritus* below. Photos by Dr. Herbert R. Axelrod.

Pseudotropheus auratus (Boulenger). A very beautiful and not uncommon fish on rocky shores, and one which exhibits remarkable sexual dimorphism; the females being gold with three horizontal black strips (including that in the dorsal fin) while in the males the ground colour is black and the horizontal bars are electric blue. Feeds on loose algae off rocks. Grows to 9 cm.

Pseudotropheus fuscus Trewavas . A rather sombrely coloured 'Mbuna' of skulking habits which lives very close to the shore-line. Not uncommon, another 'aufwuchs' feeder. Grows to 11 cm.

Pseudotropheus fuscoides Fryer . Unlike most species of *Pseudotropheus* this species feeds not on algae but on insects. Known only from a few specimens collected at Nkata Bay. Largest recorded length 9.5 cm.

Pseudotropheus novemfasciatus Regan . The type was collected by Wood, and fifteen specimens up to 9.4 cm. in the British Museum, collected by Christy, are attributed by Trewavas to this species. There are no recent data and the species may not be distinct from *Pseudotropheus tropheops.*

Pseudotropheus tropheops Regan . One of the most abundant and most variable of the 'Mbuna', feeding on both loose and attached algae. The variability extends to both structural features and colorations. Grows to about 13 cm.

GENUS *MELANOCHROMIS*

Melanochromis labrosus Trewavas . Known only from the type, collected at Deep Bay (Christy), 5.4 cm. in total length.

Melanochromis perspicax Trewavas . Known only from the type, collected at Deep Bay (Christy), 8.1 cm. in total length.

Melanochromis brevis Trewavas . Known only from two specimens from Nkudzi and Monkey Bay (Christy), the largest 12 cm. in total length.

Melanochromis melanopterus Trewavas . A fairly active carnivorous species feeding mainly on insects, though a crab, a small fish and algae have been recorded. Largest recorded size 12.9 cm. (Fryer, 1959).

Melanochromis vermivorus Trewavas . Known only from twenty-five specimens from Nkudzi (Christy), the largest 9.5 cm. in total length.

169

GENUS *GENYOCHROMIS*

Genyochromis mento Trewavas . This species has the remarkable habit of scraping large scales from other fishes, particularly *Labeo*. These scales seem to form the basis of
its diet and appear to be completely broken down in the
alimentary canal. The teeth are specially adapted to per-
mit this scale scraping to take place. Largest recorded
size 12.6 cm.

GENUS *LABIDOCHROMIS*

Labidochromis vellicans Trewavas . A small inshore dwelling
fish of rocky shores with sharp needle-like teeth which
function as minute forceps for the picking up of the insects which comprise the food of this species. Quite common. Seldom exceeds 7 cm. in length.

Labidochromis caeruleus Fryer . Closely related to the foregoing but readily recognizable by its beautiful cobalt blue
coloration. Probably a rather rare species. Largest recorded size 7.5 cm.

GENUS *COREMATODUS*

Corematodus shiranus Boulenger . A highly specialized Nyasa
endemic which mimics *Tilapia* of the *squamipinnis* group
and is parasitic on them, swimming among shoals of
Tilapia and feeding by rasping off scales from the caudal
peduncle with its broad bands of file-like teeth. Found in
small numbers among *Tilapia* shoals, in the south only.

Corematodus taeniatus Trewavas . In habits parasitic like the
preceding species, but this species is smaller and has a
different colour pattern, mimicking and preying on
Lethrinops and other cichlids which have an oblique
black band from the nape to the base of the caudal fin.

GENUS *DOCIMODUS*

Docimodus johnstoni Boulenger . An easily recognized fish
with an oblique black stripe and heavy powerful jaws with
strong cutting teeth. Taken in seines (1939 survey) and
in gill-nets off rocks. The feeding habits are still obscure.
Grows to over 25 cm. Named for Sir Harry Johnston.

GENUS *CHILOTILAPIA*

Chilotilapia rhoadesii (Boulenger). A well marked fish with two
longitudinal black bands, strikingly similar to the colour
pattern of *Haplochromis euchilus* and with large blunt
teeth. These are used to break the shells of molluscs,
which form the main food. Largest recorded length 22.5
cm.

10
Cichlids from Lake Tanganyika and Surrounding Waters

The following list of fishes has been taken from the Max Poll book *Exploration Hydrobiologique du Lac Tanganyika* (1946–1947), which was published in Brussels in 1956. Since that time there have been about two dozen new cichlids discovered, many by Pierre Brichard, who has the exclusive license (1973) for the exportation of fishes from the Burundi coast of Lake Tanganyika. For a description of the fishes listed below refer to Poll's book (written in French). The book is available by writing to Dr. Max Poll, Institut Royal des Sciences Naturelles de Belgique, Tervuren, Belgium.

Asprotilapia leptura Blgr
Aulonocranus dewindti (Blgr)
Bathybates ferox Blgr
Bathybates fasciatus Blgr
Bathybates minor Blgr
Bathybates graueri Stdr
Bathybates horni Stdr
Bathybates vittatus Blgr
Bathybates leo Poll
Boulengerochromis microlepis (Blgr)
Callochromis macrops macrops (Blgr)
Callochromis macrops melanostigma (Blgr)
Callochromis pleurospilus (Blgr)
Cardiopharynx schoutedeni Poll
Cunningtonia longiventralis Blgr
Cyathopharynx furcifer (Blgr)
Cyphotilapia frontosa (Blgr)

Ectodus descampsi Blgr
Eretmodus cyanostictus Blgr
Grammatotria lemairei Blgr
Haplochromis burtoni (Gthr)
Haplochromis horei (Gthr)
Haplochromis stappersi Poll
Haplochromis straeleni Poll
Haplochromis vanderhorsti Greenwood
Haplotaxodon microlepis Blgr
Haplotaxodon tricoti Poll
Hemibates stenosoma (Blgr)
Julidochromis ornatus Blgr
Julidochromis regani Poll
Julidochromis marlieri Poll
Lamprologus fasciatus Blgr
Lamprologus compressiceps Blgr
Lamprologus moorei Blgr
Lamprologus modestus Blgr
Lamprologus elongatus Blgr
Lamprologus furcifer Blgr
Lamprologus hecqui Blgr
Lamprologus brevis Blgr
Lamprologus tretocephalus Blgr
Lamprologus tretacanthus Blgr
Lamprologus lemairei Blgr
Lamprologus cunningtoni Blgr
Lamprologus multifasciatus Blgr
Lamprologus callipterus Blgr
Lamprologus occellatus Stdr
Lamprologus attenuatus Stdr
Lamprologus stappersi Pellegrin
Lamprologus leloupi Poll
Lamprologus meeli Poll
Lamprologus profundicola Poll
Lamprologus petricola Poll
Lamprologus toae Poll
Lamprologus wauthioni Poll
Lamprologus ornatipinnis Poll
Lamprologus kungweensis Poll
Lamprologus signatus Poll
Lamprologus savoryi savoryi Poll
Lamprologus savoryi elangatus Trew.

Lamprologus savoryi pulcher Trew. & I
Lamprologus sexfasciatus Trew. & Poll
Lamprologus christyi Trew. & Poll
Lamprologus pleuromaculatus Trew. &
Lamprologus leleupi Poll
Lamprologus niger Poll
Lestradea perspicax perspicax Poll
Lestradea perspicax stappersi Poll
Leptochromis calliurus (Blgr)
Limnochromis pfefferi (Blgr)
Limnochromis leptosoma (Blgr)
Limnochromis auritus (Blgr)
Limnochromis nigripinnis Blgr
Limnochromis otostigma Regan
Limnochromis permaxillaris David
Limnochromis christyi Trewavas
Limnochromis abeelei Poll
Limnochromis staneri Poll
Limnochromis dhanisi Poll
Limnochromis microlepidotus Poll
Limnotilapia dardennei (Blgr)
Limnotilapia trematocephala (Blgr)
Limnotilapia loocki Poll
Lobochilotes labiatus Blgr
Ophthalmochromis ventralis (Blgr)
Ophthalmotilapia boops (Blgr)
Orthochromis malagaraziensis (David)
Perissodus microlepis Blgr
Petrochromis polyodon Blgr
Petrochromis fasciolatus Blgr
Petrochromis trewavasae Poll
Plecodus paradoxus Blgr
Plecodus straeleni Poll
Plecodus elaviae Poll
Plecodus multidentatus Poll
Simochromis diagramma (Gthr)
Simochromis babaulti Pellegrin
Simochromis curvifrons Poll
Simochromis marginatus Poll
Spathodus marlieri Poll
Spathodus erythrodon Blgr
Tanganicodus irsacae Poll

Diplotaxodon ecclesi.

Telmatochromis temporalis Blgr
Telmatochromis bifrenatus Myers
Telmatochromis vittatus Blgr
Telmatochromis caninus Poll
Telmatochromis burgeoni Poll
Tilapia nilotica (Linn)
Tilapia melanopleura Dumeril
Tilapia tanganicae (Gthr)
Tilapia karomo Poll
Trematocara marginatum Blgr
Trematocara unimaculatum Blgr
Trematocara nigrifrons Blgr
Trematocara stigmaticum Poll
Trematocara caparti Poll
Trematocara kufferathi Poll
Trematocara macrostoma Poll

Trematocara variabile Poll
Tropheus moorei Blgr
Tylochromis polylepis (Blgr)
Xenochromis hecqui Blgr
Xenotilapia melanogenys (Blgr)
Xenotilapia sima Blgr
Xenotilapia ornatipinnis Blgr
Xenotilapia ochrogenys ochrogenys (Blgr)
Xenotilapia ochrogenys bathyphilus Poll
Xenotilapia boulengeri (Poll)
Xenotilapia lestradei Poll
Xenotilapia nigrolabiata Poll
Xenotilapia longispinis longispinus Poll
Xenotilapia longispinis burtoni Poll
Xenotilapia caudafasciata Poll
Xenotilapia tenuidenta Poll

Haplochromis auromarginatus.

Haplochromis chrysonotus.

Haplochromis obtusus.

Haplochromis spilonotus.

Chilotilapia rhoadesii male in normal dress.

Chilotilapia rhoadesii male in breeding color.

Head study of *Chilotilapia rhoadesii*. The indentation on the upper lip is not normal.

Haplochromis fuscotaeniatus. This fish just died of suffocation by being kept in a small container for too long a period of time.

Haplochromis labridens.

Haplochromis polystigma, male, in breeding color.

Haplochromis taeniolatus, female.

Lethrinops gossei, female.

Lethrinops aurita.

Lethrinops parvidens.

Lethrinops polli.

Lethrinops furcicauda. Below, a closeup of the anal fin.

Lethrinops furcicauda, head study. Note the fine teeth. This dentition helps them dig out the chironomid larvae on sandy beaches. It has the long, pointed face common to most dirt-eaters (similar to the South American genus *Geophagus*).

Lethrinops christyi was once considered rare. The author collected dozens of them. The fish above is a breeding male; below is a closeup of the head. On the facing page is a detail of the anal fin and the egg spots.

Lethrinops lethrinus.

Pseudotropheus, a new species to be described in a future issue of *Tropical Fish Hobbyist* magazine.

Labidochromis fryeri from Maleri Island, Lake Malawi.
Trematocranus peterdaviesi.

Pseudotropheus elegans, female above; detail of unpaired fins below.

Pseudotropheus elegans male in breeding color.

Haplochromis modestus. Photo of a dead fish by Michael Oliver.

Melanochromis auratus, male dominant color.

A male *Melanochromis melanopterus* photographed in the lobby of the Monkey Bay Hotel on Monkey Bay, Malawi.

Pseudotropheus elongatus, male above, female below.

The above color morph of *Labeotropheus trewavasae* is very rare. Both fishes (above and below) appear to be females of the same species. The one below is in the familiar OB color pattern.

The overhanging snout is characteristic of species of the genus *Labeotropheus*. Here, in *Labeotropheus trewavasae,* the normal colored male is above, and the lower fish, a female, is of the peppered or mottled variety. Lake Malawi. Photo by Dr. Herbert R. Axelrod.

An atypical strain of *Labeotropheus trewavasae*. Probably not all of the different color varieties of this species have been described yet. Lake Malawi. Photo by Dr. Herbert R. Axelrod.

Labeotropheus fuelleborni has been successfully bred in home aquaria and is one of the favorites from Lake Malawi. In this pair the male is the upper fish. Photo by Stanley Lieberman.

The female *Labeotropheus trewavasae* carries the eggs. Here the "throat" is distended with her most recent brood. Lake Malawi. Photo by H. Hansen, Aquarium Berlin.

A male *Pseudotropheus microstoma* from Lake Malawi. Photo by Dr. R.J. Goldstein.

The female *Pseudotropheus microstoma* does not differ greatly from the male. Lake Malawi. Photo by Dr. R.J. Goldstein.

This *Pseudotropheus tropheops* male is much more brightly colored than the one on page 46. Lake Malawi. Photo by Dr. Herbert R. Axelrod.

Female (above) and male (below) *Melanochromis* cf. *johanni*, commonly called "ornatus" in the trade. Likoma Island, Lake Malawi.

Pseudotropheus elongatus, male from Lake Malawi. Photo by Karl Knaack.

A male (above) and what appears to be a female (below) *Cynotilapia afra*. These were captured in Lake Malawi near Likoma Island. Photo by Dr. Herbert R. Axelrod.

One of the plainer colored *Pseudotropheus tropheops* from Lake Malawi. Similar dark patterns of the fins are present in other species of African Lake cichlids. Photo by Dr. Herbert R. Axelrod.

Two female *Melanochromis* cf. *johanni*, the males of which appear on nearby pages. Lake Malawi near Likoma Island.

Pseudotropheus tropheops, male above, female below. These fish came from Lake Malawi near Likoma Island. Photo by Dr. Herbert R. Axelrod.

A *Pseudotropheus elongatus* male in its dark phase is just as colorful as *P. zebra*. But notice the elongate, or slender, body. Lake Malawi. Photo by D. Terver, Nancy Aquarium, France.

The fishes above and below and on pages 198 and 201 may be color morphs of *Melanochromis johanni*. They differ in proportions from specimens of *M. johanni* recently collected, but not from the specimens described by Eccles. Photos of specimens from near Likoma Island, Lake Malawi.

The color changes that the lake cichlids undergo are a source of confusion. It is difficult to believe that both these fish (above and below) are the same species, *Melanochromis vermivorus.* Lake Malawi. Photos by Hilmar Hansen, Aquarium Berlin.

The female *Melanochromis vermivorus* has a pattern like that of the male, but the colors are different as can be seen in this photo. Although this species has been bred in home aquaria, such reports are few and far between. Photo by G. Marcuse.

Probably one of the more confused species is this *Iodotropheus sprengerae*, commonly known as the rust or lavender cichlid. It had been confused with *Petrotilapia tridentiger*, which apparently is a different species altogether. Photo by Dr. R.J. Goldstein.

This species has been identified as both *Melanochromis brevis* and *Pseudotropheus lucerna*. The former name would probably be a better guess. Photo by Aaron Norman.

This yellow variety of *Pseudotropheus tropheops* shows some barring which can be compared with the specimen of reverse coloration on page 46. Photo by H. Hansen, Aquarium Berlin.

Pseudotropheus tropheops from Lake Malawi. This is probably another of the subspecies commonly attributed to the *P. tropheops* complex. Photo by Klaus Paysan.

Tropheus duboisi, in contrast to *T. moorii,* is found in deeper water, and therefore does not appear in the trade very often. Lake Tanganyika. Juvenile photographed by Peter Chlupaty.

Tilapia sparrmanii has been found in the waters near Lake Malawi but as yet has not been found in the lake itself. It is omnivorous, and is one of the few nesting species in an otherwise mouthbrooding genus. Photo by Dr. R.J. Goldstein.

One of the better known fishes from Lake Tanganyika is *Tropheus moorii.* It is found in shallower water than *T. duboisi* and usually in a rocky area. Photo by Dr. Herbert R. Axelrod.

Tropheus moorii, like many other lake cichlids, is a mouthbrooder. The eggs are reported to be among the largest in the family Cichlidae. Lake Tanganyika. Photo by Dr. Herbert R. Axelrod.

Tylochromis lateralis, young specimen above, adult below, from Lake Tanganyika. Species of this genus are thought to be maternal mouthbrooders; that is, the female cares for the eggs. Photo above by Dr. Herbert R. Axelrod, photo below by Hilmar Hansen, Aquarium Berlin.

A breeding male *Aulonocara macrochir* trawled from deep water in Lake Malawi. Photo by Michael K. Oliver.

Labidochromis fryeri from Mumbo Island, Lake Malawi. This is the typical coloration although the dark anal fin band is generally more blackish. Photo by H. Hansen, Aquarium Berlin.

This specimen of *Julidochromis* appears intermediate between *J. ornatus* and *J. transcriptus,* casting some doubt as to the validity of the latter species. Lake Tanganyika. Photo by Hilmar Hansen, Aquarium Berlin.

The complicated patterns in the fins and on the head make *Julidochromis marlieri* easy to recognize. It reaches a larger size than other species in the genus. Photo by Dr. R. J. Goldstein.

One of the more popular of African lake cichlids, *Lamprologus brichardi*. This fish used to go under the name *Lamprologus savoryi elongatus* but Dr. Max Poll has discovered that that name can no longer be used for this fish. The other *Lamprologus*, *L. savoryi savoryi*, will remain unchanged. Photo by H.J. Richter.

Lamprologus brichardi has been spawned in captivity as this and the following photos show. The male, to the left, is reported to have slightly longer finnage than the female. Photo by H.J. Richter.

The male approaches close to the female so that he can take position by her side as the eggs are laid, because he fertilizes them at the moment of extrusion. Photo by H.J. Richter.

The male and female undergo many different maneuvers during the actual spawning. Here the camera caught them in an unusual pose. Photo by H.J. Richter.

The site selected is usually a smooth rock such as those in the background. Photo by H.J. Richter.

The first eggs are visible on the gray rock in the lower right hand corner of the photo. Photo by H.J. Richter.

Spawning continues, and more eggs will be deposited on the spawning site in due time. Photo by H.J. Richter.

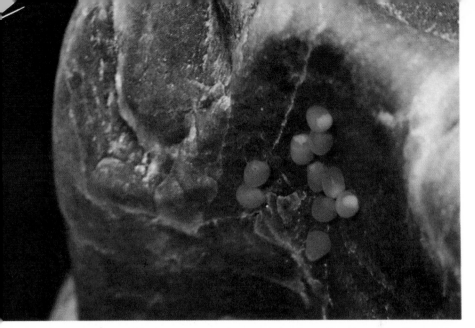

The eggs are fairly large, amber colored, and adhere to the rock. Photo by H.J. Richter.

This *Lamprologus compressiceps* appears quite different from *L. brichardi* but are placed in the same genus. Photo by W. Hoppe.

Occasional imports include some of the other species of *Lamprologus*, such as *L. attenuatus*. It is a bottom nester from Lake Tanganyika. Photo by Dr. R.J. Goldstein.

Telmatochromis temporalis has often been confused with *Lamprologus petricola*, but *L. petricola* is a dark fish. The blue streak across the cheek appears to identify *temporalis*. Photo by Aaron Norman.

This specimen of *Haplochromis spilostichus* was trawled from 10-16 fathoms (60-100 feet) off Chembe village, Malawi. Photo by Michael K. Oliver.

A frequenter of the sandy shores of Lake Malawi is *Haplochromis strigatus.* Photo by Michael K. Oliver.

After examination of the specimens pictured, these fish turned out to be a new species and have been described as *Melanochromis exasperatus*. The upper fish is a young male and the lower photo is of a ripe female. Both came from Likoma Island, Lake Malawi. Photos by Dr. Herbert R. Axelrod.

A mixed group of cichlids from Lake Malawi. Upper fish is probably *Melanochromis perspicax*, center fish is a female *Labeotropheus fuelleborni*, and the lower fish is *Haplochromis livingstoni*. Photo by G. Marcuse.

Haplochromis venustus is a carnivorous cichlid from Lake Malawi which may be found in sandy areas and in grass beds. Photo by G. Marcuse.

A young *Haplochromis fuscotaeniatus* showing a color pattern similar to that of the adult (see p. 178). Photo by Warren E. Burgess.

The sulphur yellow nape is clearly visible on this *Haplochromis venustus*. Photo by Dr. Herbert R. Axelrod at the Berlin Aquarium.

One of the newer imports from Lake Malawi, the peacock blue cichlid. Specimens of this beautiful *Aulanocara nyassae* are hard to come by. Photo by Aaron Norman.

Hemitilapia oxyrhynchus is a browser among *Vallisneria* beds, scraping algae and insects from the leaves. Photo by Dr. Herbert R. Axelrod at the Berlin Aquarium.

Haplochromis sp. (possibly *H. jacksoni*). One must see this fish "in person" to appreciate its beauty. Photo by G. Marcuse.

One of the large-mouthed species, *Serranochromis robustus.* The dark lateral stripe is common to several species of Lake Malawi cichlids.

A species that often appears for sale is *Melanochromis perspicax* from Lake Malawi. This is a female. Photo by Warren E. Burgess.

The highly developed lips of this *Melanochromis labrosus* may be sensory in nature for the detection of food. Photo by Aaron Norman.

Males of many of the cichlids are often more colorful than the females. Although the upper individual of this pair of *Melanochromis brevis* was identified as a female and the lower one a male, I am inclined to think that the opposite is true. Photos by Warren E. Burgess.

Lobochilotes labiatus has also developed expanded or thickened lips, but apparently independently from *Melano-chromis labrosus*. Photo by G. Marcuse.

←————

Melanochromis melanopterus is closely related to *M. ver-mivorus* and there has been confusion as to the identity of these two species. Photo by Dr. Herbert R. Axelrod.

Melanochromis simulans(?) has a longer snout than *M. vermivorus*, but the color pattern is very similar (see pp. 204-5). Photo by G. Marcuse.

Not all of the African cichlids are big and heavy bodied. This slender *Limnochromis nigripinnis* is from Lake Tanganyika. Photo by Warren E. Burgess.

Telmatochromis vittatus is very close to and may be confused with *T. bifrenatus*. Individuals of the fish pictured here may be sold under either name. Photo by Warren E. Burgess.

A female (above) and male (below) *Melanochromis exasperatus* (often incorrectly referred to as *Labidochromis joanjohnsonae*). This species is very popular with aquarists. Photo by Dr. Herbert R. Axelrod.

A new *Labidochromis* from Mumbo Island. Many Lake Malawi cichlids have this color pattern, but no other *Labidochromis*. Photo by Warren. E. Burgess.

An unidentified species of *Labidochromis* from Chisumulu Island, Lake Malawi. Photo by Warren E. Burgess.

The Likoma Island morph of a male *Melanochromis johanni* differs somewhat in pattern from the specimen shown on p. 48. Photo by Warren E. Burgess.

A female of the Likoma Island morph of *Melanochromis johanni.* No specific differences are apparent between this one and the female on p. 48. Photo by Warren E. Burgess.

The female *Pseudotropheus tropheops gracilior* shown here lacks the egg spots of the male. Photo by Warren E. Burgess.

The male *Pseudotropheus tropheops gracilior* is much more colorful than the female above. Photo by Warren E. Burgess.

Cynotilapia afra looks to all intents and purposes like *Pseudotropheus zebra*. In *Cynotilapia* the teeth are unicuspid, but in *Pseudotropheus* they are bicuspid.

A colorful *Cynotilapia* species from the Mozambique shores of Lake Malawi. Photo by Warren E. Burgess.

Lamprologus brichardi with some of the young swimming nearby. The small fish develop white edges to the caudal fin at an early age and look very much like the adults. Photo by H.J. Richter.

Spawns of African Rift Lake cichlids are generally small compared to the hundreds of eggs laid by other cichlids. One or two dozen fry are considered a successful spawn. Photo by H.J. Richter.

Another color variety of *Pseudotropheus zebra*. More morphs have been reported from Lake Malawi and may soon show up in the retail stores. Photo by G. Marcuse.

Pseudotropheus tropheops gracilior female from Likoma
Island, Lake Malawi. Photo by Warren E. Burgess.

Trematocranus jacobfreibergi is a recent import from Lake
Malawi. Photo by Dr. Herbert R. Axelrod.

Petrotilapia tridentiger is probably one of the largest of the mbunas. It also extends to a depth of over 200 feet and is likely limited in depth only by the lack of oxygen. Photo by Warren E. Burgess.

Labidochromis sp. from Chisumulu Island similar to that on p. 237 (top). Photo by Warren E. Burgess.

Labidochromis fryeri is less colorful than some of the other Lake Malawi cichlids. Photo by Warren E. Burgess.

The caudal fin pattern of *Pseudotropheus lanisticola* is very distinctive for an mbuna.

This laterally flattened species is *Haplochromis compressi-ceps*. It has received the common name Malawian eye-biter because of its habit of including the eyes of other fishes in its diet. The full-bodied view (above) and the close up of the head (below) give little indication of the extent of the compression of the body. Photos by Dr. Herbert R.Axelrod at the Berlin Aquarium.

The dark bars on this *Pseudotropheus* sp. have faded somewhat but this fish appears to be the one called "dingani" by aquarists. Photo by Hans J. Richter.

One of the *Pseudotropheus zebra*-like species which often goes under the trade name "dingani." Photo by Dr. Herbert R. Axelrod.

One of the newer imports is this tangerine *Pseudotropheus zebra*. Photo by G. Marcuse.

A very young *Pseudotropheus*, possibly *P. zebra*. The full color of the adult is not attained until later in its life. Photo by H.J. Richter.

A male *Pseudotropheus* sp. Note the long pelvic fins. Photo by Dr. Herbert R. Axelrod.

The female *Pseudotropheus* sp. incubates the eggs in her mouth. In the upper photo she is picking them up from the aquarium gravel where they were laid. In the lower photo she has finished, as indicated by her extended buccal area. This fish and the male opposite are often called "dingani."

Pseudotropheus tropheops variety from Likoma Island, Lake Malawi. Male. Photo by Warren E. Burgess.

A female of the *Pseudotropheus tropheops* variety from Likoma Island. Photo by Warren E. Burgess.

One of the color varieties of *Pseudotropheus tropheops*.
This color polymorphism causes considerable confusion in
African lake cichlid taxonomy. Photo by G. Marcuse.

African Rift Lake cichlids can be quite rough in an aquarium leaving some individuals in as sorry a state as this *Haplochromis longimanus*. Always provide plenty of cover to reduce losses. Photo by Dr. Herbert R. Axelrod.

Species of *Rhamphochromis* are predators, feeding on cich-lids of the "Utaka" group and *Engraulicypris sardella*, a cyprinid.

Lamprologus compressiceps received its name due to the highly compressed nature of its head. Photo courtesy Wardley Products Co.

A very colorful individual of *Iodotropheus sprengerae*. Only a few color morphs of this species have been imported. Photo by Stanislav Frank.

One of the more common color phases of *Iodotropheus sprengerae*. Notice it has the same pattern as the fish in the photo above. Photo by Jaroslav Elias.

A male (darker fish) and a female *Melanochromis parallelus,* which is currently known in the trade as the black-
and-white auratus. Photo by Dr. Herbert R. Axelrod.

A group of male *Melanochromis* sp., probably *M. johanni,*
with a red and a normal *Pseudotropheus zebra* nearby.
Photo by Dr. Herbert R. Axelrod at the Berlin Aquarium.

A male (darker fish at back) and female (yellow fish) *Labeotropheus trewavasae*. The golden *trewavasae* are becoming very popular at this time. Photo by Dr. Herbert R. Axelrod.

A mottled **male** *Labeotropheus trewavasae*. This is the famous 'marmalade cat' and is apparently quite rare. Photo by Dr. Herbert R. Axelrod.

The normal male *Labeotropheus trewavasae* is quite an attractive fish and has become one of the most popular of the mbunas. Photo courtesy Wardley Products Co.

A normal mottled female *Labeotropheus trewavasae*. This one was found to be ripe with eggs. Note how closely it resembles the male marmalade cat opposite. Photo by Dr. Herbert R. Axelrod.

Labidochromis fryeri is readily recognizable by color and pattern as well as tooth characteristics. Its teeth, however, differ somewhat from the typical species of *Labidochromis*. Photo by Dr. Herbert R. Axelrod.

Although similar in pattern to *Labidochromis fryeri*, this fish (*Pseudotropheus* sp.) has different color and tooth characteristics. Photo by Dr. Herbert R. Axelrod.

This appears to be a male *Melanochromis exasperatus* in the dominant color phase. The orange striping is mostly hidden by the overall bluish color. Photo by H.J. Richter.

The female *Labidochromis textilis* is distinguishable in an aquarium from *Melanochromis exasperatus* females by the more numerous and more even horizontal stripes. Photo by Dr. Bruce J. Turner.

Labidochromis mathothoi, male above, female below. This is one of the less colorful species of *Labidochromis* as yet discovered and rarely, if ever, is imported.

Pseudotropheus minutus is shaped something like a *Labidochromis* but does not have the tooth structure of species of that genus.

Two male *Labidochromis vellicans*. The relatively shallow
body, which is quite visible here, is one of the characteristics
of the species.

Labidochromis sp., a brightly colored mbuna from Lake
Malawi.

This bright blue mbuna goes under a number of names (*Pseudotropheus "eduardi," P. "pindani,"* and *P. socolofi*), none of which may be valid. This species does not exhibit sexual dimorphism. Photo by Dr. Herbert R. Axelrod.

The shape of the snout is distinctive in this pair of recently described mbuna, *Pseudotropheus tursiops*. The female is the top fish. Photo by Dr. Herbert R. Axelrod.

Pseudotropheus aurora is another recently described species that is recognizable by its large eye and bright yellow antero-ventral area. Photo by Dr. Herbert R. Axelrod.

The uncommon white male *Pseudotropheus zebra* still commands a relatively high price. Photo by Dr. Herbert R. Axelrod.

This female *Pseudotropheus zebra* morph had 19 ripe eggs in the right ovary. The color is unusual for zebras. Photo by Dr. Herbert R. Axelrod.

This mottled female *Pseudotropheus tropheops* has a
background color similar to that of the female zebra on the
opposite page. Photo by Dr. Herbert R. Axelrod.

A bright yellow morph of *Pseudotropheus tropheops* is becoming more common in the aquarium trade. Photo by Dr.
Herbert R. Axelrod.

Petrotilapia tridentiger looks very much like a zebra in color pattern but can be recognized by looking at the mouth. Two males and a female (light colored fish) can be seen here. Photo by Dr. Robert Goldstein.

The teeth of *Petrotilapia tridentiger* are all tricuspid in contrast to species of the genus *Pseudotropheus* where the outer row is bicuspid. Photo by Dr. Herbert R. Axelrod.

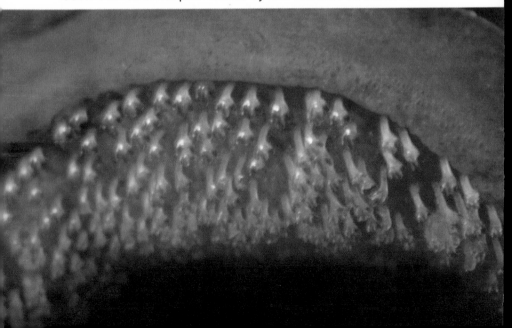

A very beautiful color morph of *Cynotilapia afra*. Notice the resemblance of this species to *Pseudotropheus zebra* below. Photo by Dr. Herbert R. Axelrod.

Pseudotropheus zebra is now one of the mainstays of the African cichlid aquarium trade. It is often the first fish kept by those who want to start on the African lake cichlids. Photo by Dr. Herbert R. Axelrod.

A pair of *Telmatochromis caninus* guarding eggs laid under a
flat rock. Photo by H.J. Richter.

Lamprologus tretocephalus is often confused with young
Cyphotilapia frontosa although details of the banding are different.

Male *Pseudotropheus* sp. (called "kenyi" or "lilancinius" in the trade) with its golden color, a reverse of most *Pseudotropheus* species. Photo by Ed Isaacs, Pet Gallery.

The female *Pseudotropheus* sp. is blue, also a reverse of the normal situation of male and female species of *Pseudotropheus*. Photo by Ed Isaacs, Pet Gallery.

Lamprologus elongatus from Lake Tanganyika. Photo by H. Scheuermann.

A spawning pair of *Lamprologus elongatus* with their most recent brood. Note the typical rocks-only African lake cichlid tank. Photo by H. Scheuermann.

Spathodus erythrodon. The characteristic blue spots are faint-ly visible on the body and have turned dark on the head in this frightened individual.

The shape of the body and head of goby-cichlids, like this *Eretmodus cyanostictus,* indicates a bottom type existence. Photo courtesy Wardley Products Co.

The great development of the hump in *Haplochromis moorii* is shown in this close-up photo. Photo by Michael Oliver.

This young *Haplochromis moorii*, as shown here, is more normal in appearance although the first indications of the hump can be seen. Photo by Dr. Herbert R. Axelrod.

Red-top zebra, *Pseudotropheus zebra*. This is one of the many colorful morphs of *P. zebra* and is very popular in the hobby.

The horizontal stripes and barred caudal fin make *Julidochromis regani* easily recognizable. Photo by Thierry Brichard.

Julidochromis transcriptus is very dark and has been called the masked *Julidochromis*. Photo by Thierry Brichard.

The second most popular species of *Julidochromis* (after *J. ornatus*) is *J. marlieri*. It is often available in aquarium stores dealing with African cichlids. Photo by Thierry Brichard.

There are several varieties of *Julidochromis* which are hard to place with any particular species. This one may be a pale form of *J. marlieri*. Photo by Thierry Brichard.

Several species of Lake Tanganyika cichlids are often confused. *Triglachromis otostigma* (formerly *Limnochromis otostigma*) was often mistaken for *Limnochromis auritus*. Photo by Homer Arment.

Limnochromis auritus resembles *T. otostigma* but has longitudinal light bluish stripes instead of diagonal ones. Photo by Dr. R.J. Goldstein.

This Lake Tanganyika fish is *Xenotilapia melanogenys*, one of the less common forms that rarely appear for sale. Photo by Aaron Norman.

Callochromis pleurospilus is one of the more colorful of the Lake Tanganyika fishes, but it has not gained very much in popularity. Photo by Dr. Herbert R. Axelrod.

The Malawian scale-eater, *Genyochromis mento*; females have this typical blotched color pattern. Photo by A. Ivanoff.

The male Malawian scale-eater. The common name is well deserved, and not many tank-mates are safe from its attacks. Photo by A. Ivanoff.

The Malawi peacock, *Aulonocara nyassae,* is one of the most popular Lake Malawi cichlids. The male shown here is from a population which lacks the orange shoulder area. Photo by Warren E. Burgess.

Females and young males of *Aulonocara nyassae* exhibit a striped pattern. Photo by Warren E. Burgess.

The large "egg" spots in the anal fin are clearly visible in *Haplochromis callipterus*. Photo by Dr. Herbert R. Axelrod.

One of the larger species of *Haplochromis* is *H. woodi*. Photo by Dr. Herbert R. Axelrod.

Some species of *Haplochromis* are more brightly colored than some of the mbunas. This one is *H. similis*. Photo by Dr. Herbert R. Axelrod.

Though obviously a male, this fish has none of the so-called "egg" spots in the anal fin. The orange spots in the dorsal fin, however, do resemble cichlid eggs in both size and color. Photo by Dr. Herbert R. Axelrod.

A young *Haplochromis rostratus*. The pattern of spots is characteristic, as is an extended snout which develops as the fish grows. Photo by Dr. Herbert R. Axelrod.

The large fleshy lips are well developed in this *Haplochromis euchilus* from Lake Malawi. Photo by Dr. Herbert R. Axelrod.

Haplochromis ericotaenia from Lake Malawi. Many of the *Haplochromis* species have this silvery color with blackish markings. Photo by Michael K. Oliver.

A young *Haplochromis fenestratus* in its fright color pattern. Photo by Dr. Robert J. Goldstein.

A close-up of the characteristic snout of *Haplochromis linni* from Lake Malawi. Photo by Dr. Herbert R. Axelrod.

A comparison photo showing two speckled species, *Haplochromis linni* (above) and *H. polystigma* (below). Photo by Dr. Herbert R. Axelrod.

Haplochromis johnstoni, one of the vertically barred cichlids from Lake Malawi. Photo by G. Meola, African Fish Imports.

Haplochromis polystigma in a typical "yawning" pose. Photo by G. Meola, African Fish Imports.

Lamprologus tretocephalus. The dark bars extend into the dorsal fin here to a greater extent than in the other specimens pictured, possibly due to age. Photo by H. Scheuermann.

Lamprologus tretocephalus is often confused with *L. sexfasciatus*, but has only three bars below the dorsal fin in comparison with four for *sexfasciatus*. Photo by G. Meola, African Fish Imports.

A group of small *L. tretocephalus* in a basically rock-decorated African cichlid tank. Photo by G. Meola, African Fish Imports.

The young spotted form of *Tropheus duboisi* from Lake Tanganyika.

With age the spots of *Tropheus duboisi* disappear.

The typical *Tropheus moorii* male is dark with a band of color (red, yellow, white, etc.) across the body behind the pectoral fin.

Several new morphs of *Tropheus moorii* have appeared recently, including this striped form.

Chalinochromis brichardi. The striped pattern of the juvenile breaks up into spots that eventually disappear in the adults. Photo by G. Meola, African Fish Imports.

Chalinochromis sp. bears a close resemblance to the recently described *Julidochromis dickfeldi.* Photo by G. Meola, African Fish Imports.

The markings of the head of *Chalinochromis brichardi* are quite distinctive. Note the extra stripe behind the eye (lacking in *Chalinochromis* sp.) and the lower jaw teeth.

Adult and near adult *Chalinochromis brichardi.* Even the last dorsal spot may eventually disappear.

Julidochromis regani. The fin pattern of this individual has all but disappeared.

Diplotaxodon argenteus has been captured at depths of 30-40 meters where it feeds on other fishes, mainly *Engraulocypris.*

The golden form of *Lamprologus leleupi.* This species should not be confused with *L. leloupi,* an entirely different fish.

Haplochromis fuscotaeniatus male from Lake Malawi in spawning coloration. Photo by G. Meola, African Fish Imports.

Lamprologus compressiceps of Lake Tanganyika. Note the proportionately large mouth.

Petrochromis polyodon, probably a female with shorter fins.

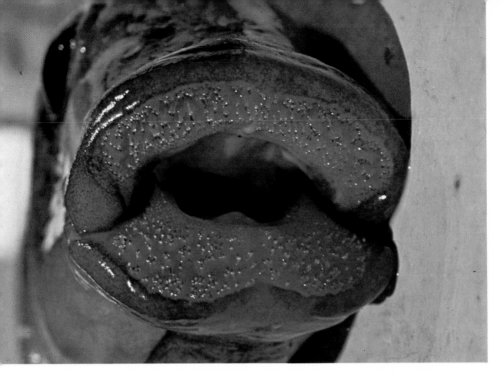

Closeup of the mouth and teeth of *Petrochromis polyodon*. Note the similarity between the teeth of this species and *Petrotilapia tridentiger* of Lake Malawi (p. 270).

Adult male *Petrochromis polyodon* with filaments on the un-paired and pelvic fins. Note also the "egg-spots" in the dorsal and anal fins.

Haplochromis modestus male in breeding color. Compare this with the fish on p. 189. Photo by Warren E. Burgess.

Haplochromis sp. (possibly *H. woodi*). The position of the dark spots along the side and back is characteristic. Photo by Warren E. Burgess.

Above and below: Trematocranus sp. This fish has been sold under the trade name "Red-Top *Aristochromis*" even though there is no resemblance at all between *Trematocranus* and the true *Aristochromis*. Photos by G. Meola, African Fish Imports.

Haplochromis of the *modestus*-complex, dark male. Photo by Warren E. Burgess.

Non-dominant male *Haplochromis* of the *modestus*-complex, presumably the same species as the above. Photo by Warren E. Burgess.

Lethrinops sp. Still as yet unidentified and possibly a new species. Photo by Warren E. Burgess.

Haplochromis sp. Breeding male, possibly *H. mollis* or another diagonally striped *Haplochromis*. Photo by Warren E. Burgess.

Young male *Trematocranus jacobfreibergi* just starting to develop some of the coloring of the adult male. Photo by Warren E. Burgess.

Female *Trematocranus jacobfreibergi* are banded and not very colorful. Photo by Warren E. Burgess.

Adult male *Trematocranus jacobfreibergi* in dark breeding color. The stripes are barely discernible.

Adult male *Trematocranus jacobfreibergi* in a lighter color phase than the one above. Photo by G. Meola, African Fish Imports.

The juvenile *Pseudotropheus elegans* shown here is very similar to the adults shown on previous pages. Photo by Warren E. Burgess.

Cynotilapia afra, "eduardi" form with the striped dorsal. This fish was a ripe male. Photo by Warren E. Burgess.

Cynotilapia axelrodi female has less intense color than the male. This female was nearly ripe. Photo by Warren E. Burgess.

Cynotilapia axelrodi, male. The anal fin color might serve to distinguish the male from the female of this species. Photo by Warren E. Burgess.

Labidochromis vellicans was the first species of *Labidochromis* to be discovered and named. Photo by Warren E. Burgess.

Labidochromis fryeri diverges slightly from the basic *Labidochromis* stock by having weakly bicuspid teeth. Photo by Warren E. Burgess.

The true *Labidochromis caeruleus* has dark stripes in the dorsal and anal fins. Photo by Warren E. Burgess.

Another phase of *Labidochromis caeruleus* with less blue. Both this fish and the one above are males. Photo by Warren E. Burgess.

Above and below: Pseudotropheus (or *Labidochromis*) *minutus.* The above specimen has more bars and the specimen below has indications of a dorsal fin stripe, but both appear to be the same species. Photo above by Warren E. Burgess; photo below by G. Meola, African Fish Imports.

Above and below: Labidochromis sp. The male (above) is darker and generally more colorful than the female (below). Both of these fishes were ripe when captured. Photos by Warren E. Burgess.

A relatively new importation, the black-top fuelleborni. Many new varieties of *Labeotropheus fuelleborni* are still being discovered. Photo by Warren E. Burgess.

One of the popular varieties of *Labeotropheus fuelleborni* is the orange-sided fuelleborni shown here.

The very colorful OB or orange blotched *Labeotropheus fuelle-borni* is almost always a female. Photo by Warren E. Burgess.

Occasionally an OB male *Labeotropheus fuelleborni* is found and can be recognized by the bluish tints on the body. It is called the marmalade cat just as the OB male of *L. trewavasae* is. Photo by G. Meola, African Fish Imports.

Pseudotropheus sp. This fish is called "jacksoni" in the trade.
Photo by G. Meola, African Fish Imports.

Pseudotropheus sp. In addition to the names given on p. 266,
this species is also commonly called "newsi" in the trade.
Photo by G. Meola, African Fish Imports.

Pseudotropheus sp. This *P. zebra*-like species has a very unusual color and the teeth differ from those of the true *P. zebra.*
Photo by Warren E. Burgess.

Pseudotropheus zebra, mottled variety. This seems to be a
variation of the OB zebra female. Photo by Warren E. Burgess.

Pseudotropheus microstoma, dark phase. The steeply descending snout marks this as a member of the *P. tropheops* complex. Photo by Warren E. Burgess.

Pseudotropheus sp. No definite identification of this fish has yet been determined.

This is a photograph of the holotype of the shell-dwelling species *Pseudotropheus lanisticola*. Photo by Warren E. Burgess.

This large-lipped *Haplochromis* sp. (probably a breeding male *H. euchilus*) has affectionately been called the "Super VC-10" (after the jet plane) by Peter Davies. Photo by Warren E. Burgess.

Pseudotropheus sp. of the *P. elongatus*-complex. This species has been called various names in the trade, the most recent being "bentoni." Photo by Warren E. Burgess.

Pseudotropheus elongatus is a very slender bodied mbuna and can be easily identified. Photo by Warren E. Burgess.

Melanochromis vermivorus male in breeding color. Note the whitish dorsal fin. Photo by Warren E. Burgess.

Melanochromis parallelus male. The dorsal fin is dark in this species and the lateral stripes are bluish, here blending into the dark background of the fish. Photo by Warren E. Burgess.

Female *Melanochromis* "chipokae" (above) and male of the same species (below) showing the typical *Melanochromis* patterns, dark stripes on a light background in the female and light stripes on a dark background in the male. Photos by G. Meola, African Fish Imports.

Simochromis curvifrons. Photo by Glen Axelrod.

Simochromis marginatus. Photo by Glen Axelrod.

Cyathopharynx furcifer. Photo by Glen Axelrod.

Telmatochromis bifrenatus. Photo by Glen Axelrod.

Lobochilotes labiatus. Photo by Glen Axelrod.

Lobochilotes labiatus. Head photo by Glen Axelrod.

Tanganicodus irsacae. Photo by Glen Axelrod.
Tanganicodus irsacae. Color phase. Photo by Glen Axelrod.

Eretmodus cyanostictus. Photo by Glen Axelrod.
Spathodus erythrodon. Photo by Glen Axelrod.

Petrochromis polyodon. Photo by Glen Axelrod.

Petrochromis sp. Photo by Glen Axelrod.

Petrochromis sp. Photo by Glen Axelrod.

Petrochromis sp. Photo by Glen Axelrod.

Limnochromis leptosoma. Photo by Glen Axelrod.
Limnochromis leptosoma. Males and females. Photo by Glen Axelrod.

Julidochromis regani. Southern form. Photo by Glen Axelrod.

Ophthalmochromis ventralis. Photo by Glen Axelrod.

Haplochromis burtoni. Photo by Glen Axelrod.
Haplochromis burtoni. Fin patterns. Photo by Glen Axelrod.

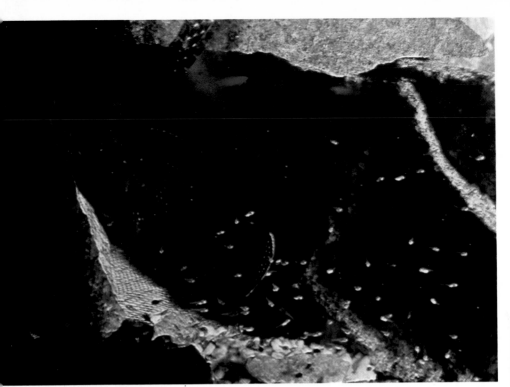

Lamprologus tetracanthus. With young. Photo by Glen Axelrod.

Lamprologus tetracanthus. Photo by Glen Axelrod.

Haplochromis horei. Photo by Glen Axelrod.

Haplochromis horei. Female. Photo by Glen Axelrod.

Haplochromis horei. Head pattern. Photo by Glen Axelrod.

Lamprologus fasciatus. Photo by Glen Axelrod.

Tropheus moorii. Red form. Photo by Glen Axelrod.

Tropheus moorii. Red form from south. Photo by Glen Axelrod.

Tropheus moorii. Yellow-belly form. Photo by Glen Axelrod.
Tropheus moorii. Form from Kigoma. Photo by Glen Axelrod.

Tropheus moorii. Brown form. Photo by Glen Axelrod.

Tropheus moorii. Green form. Photo by Glen Axelrod.

Tropheus moorii. Yellow form. Photo by Glen Axelrod.
Tropheus moorii. Fry. Photo by Glen Axelrod.

Tropheus duboisi. Narrow olive band. Photo by Glen Axelrod.
Tropheus duboisi. Wide olive band. Photo by Glen Axelrod.

Tropheus duboisi. White band. Photo by Glen Axelrod.

Tropheus duboisi. White band. Photo by Glen Axelrod.

Lamprologus compressiceps. Red form. Photo by Glen Axelrod.

Lamprologus compressiceps. Red form. Photo by Glen Axelrod.

Lamprologus compressiceps. Yellow. Photo by Glen Axelrod.

Lamprologus lemairei. Photo by Glen Axelrod.
Lamprologus furcifer. Photo by Glen Axelrod.

Lamprologus tretocephalus. With young. Photo by G. Axelrod.
Lamprologus tretocephalus. With young. Photo by Glen Axelrod.

Pseudotropheus sp. Photo by Glen Axelrod.

Pseudotropheus sp. Lake Malawi. Photo by Glen Axelrod.

Perissodus straeleni. Photo by Glen Axelrod.

Perissodus straeleni. Head pattern. Photo by Glen Axelrod.

Limnochromis sp. Photo by Glen Axelrod.
Haplochromis sp. Photo by Glen Axelrod.

Sarotherodon tanganicae. Photo by Glen Axelrod.
Tilapia nilotica. Photo by Glen Axelrod.

Tropheus sp. Photo by Glen Axelrod.

Spathodus erythrodon. Photo by Glen Axelrod.

Haplochromis sp. Photo by Glen Axelrod.

Haplochromis sp. Photo by Glen Axelrod.

Aulonocranus dewindti. Photo by Glen Axelrod.

Xenotilapia longispinis longispinis. Photo by G. Axelrod.

Lamprologus sp. Photo by Glen Axelrod.

Lamprologus sp. Photo by Glen Axelrod.

*Petrochromis
polyodon.*
Photo by
Glen Axelrod.

Petrochromis polyodon. Photo by Glen Axelrod.

Labeotropheus fuelleborni. The male above has orange tips on his fins. The female, below, has the same color pattern as the normal color of *L. trewavasae* and they are frequently confused.

The top fish is a male *Labeotropheus trewavasae,* the lower fish is an OB female morph. Photos by Dr. D. Terver at the Nancy Aquarium.

Labeotropheus fuelleborni fry above and adult male below.
Photographs by Dr. D. Terver at the Nancy Aquarium.

Plecodus paradoxus.

Cyphotilapia frontosa.

Petrochromis polyodon.

Spathodus erythrodon.

Callochromis macrops melanostigma.

Haplochromis horei.

Callochromis pleurospilus, female above, male below.

Limnotilapia dardennei.

Perissodus microlepis.

Simochromis babaulti.

Simochromis diagramma.

Limnochromis auritus.

Xenotilapia sima.

Haplochromis pfefferi.

Xenotilapia boulengeri.

Lobochilotes labiatus, head study above; side view below.

Sarotherodon tanganicae, about 18 inches long, bought at the Bujumburu fish market. Somehow the fly landed while the photo was being taken.

Telmatochromis vittatus.

Telmatochromis caninus.

Head study of *Telmatochromis caninus*.

Lamprologus callipterus, female above, male below. The plants in all photographs in this book (except those taken in aquaria) are authentic and are found with the fishes in the same lake.

Lamprologus brichardi.

Lamprologus savoryi.

Lamprologus leleupi.

Lamprologus modestus.

Lamprologus tetracanthus.

Lamprologus modestus.

Lamprologus cunningtoni.

Lamprologus elongatus.

Haplochromis moorii from Lake Malawi is not closely related to *Cyphotilapia frontosa* of Lake Tanganyika, even though they are similar in general shape. Their living colors are quite distinct. This fish is *H. moorii.*

Telmatochromis caninus, closeup of the head. The line running from the bottom of the eye is usually much blacker.

Telmatochromis temporalis, closeup of the head.

Haplochromis heterotaenia.

Haplochromis woodi. Photo by Michael Oliver.

Eretmodus cyanostictus.

Haplochromis epichorialis. Photo by Michael Oliver.

Haplochromis fenestratus male in almost complete breeding dress. Photo by Michael Oliver.

Haplochromis euchilus, female. Photo by Hilmar Hansen, Berlin Aquarium.

Haplochromis mloto, male above, female below. Note egg-spots on female's anal fin.

Haplochromis chrysonotus.

Haplochromis lepturus.

Limnochromis auritus, a close-up of the head of a breeding male. Photo by Dr. Herbert R. Axelrod.

Telmatochromis temporalis.

Cyphotilapia frontosa, just starting to get the lump on its forehead. Photo by Hilmar Hansen, Aquarium Berlin.

ILLUSTRATIONS INDEX

* The changing of *Pseudotropheus auratus* and *Pseudotropheus johanni* to *Melanochromis auratus* and *Melanochromis johanni* respectively was made too late to incorporate it into the previous editions of this book and therefore these species may still be captioned under the old names on some pages.